DATE DUE

PAGES FROM THE PAST

PAGES FROM THE PAST

---★---

By

HERBERT ALBERT LAURENS FISHER

Essay Index Reprint Series

BOOKS FOR LIBRARIES PRESS
FREEPORT, NEW YORK

First Published 1939
Reprinted 1969

STANDARD BOOK NUMBER:
8369-1260-8

LIBRARY OF CONGRESS CATALOG CARD NUMBER:
75-90638

PRINTED IN THE UNITED STATES OF AMERICA

PREFACE

I SPARE the gentle Reader my numerous educational homilies and the excursions which from time to time I have made into the fields of literary criticism. What is here obtruded on his notice is a modest sheaf of occasional papers, mainly relating to topics of historical or biographical interest, and conveying, as I would fain believe, at this time of sombre apprehension, a gentle invitation to humane studies and a rebuke to the menacing barbarism of our age. Of these pieces the most substantial is the Raleigh lecture on 'The Whig Historians', delivered to the British Academy, and the most instructive, seeing that the shifting lights and shades of an undulating and diverse nature are best displayed in a setting of fancy, the imaginary picture of Napoleon in America with which the volume opens. An address delivered to an American audience at the Lowell Institute at Boston records the impression made upon an English visitor by the American scene during that interval of golden plenty and overweening confidence which divided the close of the Great War from the financial crash of 1929. Those were days when the grim spectre of widespread unemployment had not yet arisen to haunt the conscience of the American people, when Franklin Roosevelt was still a private citizen, and when an American statesman proclaiming the urgent need for a new deal to redistribute private fortunes within the Commonwealth would have been regarded as a candidate for political suicide. The Republican star was in the ascendant. A strange

enthusiasm surged round the dry laconic little figure
of Calvin Coolidge, whose return to the White House
by a mammoth 'plurality' sent New York Centrals
up eight points and brought indescribable comfort
to the investing public.

Other papers touch on contemporary English
politics. Believing as I do that the prime source of
evil in the world to-day is the eclipse of Liberalism
(using that word not in any narrow party sense but
as denoting an attachment grounded on reason to
civil, religious, and political freedom), I have endeavoured to illustrate some aspects of the liberal
temperament in politics. For this reason I have included, together with a general address on our politicians, who, whatever their party allegiance may be,
are resolute to defend the essential fabric of their
country's liberty, some slight sketches of certain
English statesmen, who, though wearing different
party colours, were all in their several measures
servants of humanity and freedom.

Two papers are concerned with Oxford. The first,
inspired by Dr. Gunther's admirable volumes, describes that brilliant flowering of scientific curiosity
which glorified Oxford on the eve of the Restoration
and then with the formation of the Royal Society
discovered under august patronage a more natural
centre in London. The second shows how, despite
all the transformations of time and fashion, a medieval
College custom, such as the annual progress of the
Warden of New College and his outrider, may sur-
vive into our own age.

Finally, there is praise of the beauty of England.

In Oxford and its neighbourhood where so much has been done amiss, where there have been so many defacements, where the old silver-grey city of spires and towers shrinks to the size of a small jewel at the heart of a sprawling reticulation of villa residences and artisan dwellings, where peace retreats before petrol, so that only at early dawn or in brief reposeful spaces of the night is it possible to have release from the pitiless rage of the new traffic and to recapture the sweet stillness and seclusion of the past, many of us feel that an effort, far greater and more comprehensive than any which has yet been attempted, is now urgently required to save our national inheritance. I am glad to think that the Oxford Preservation Trust is alive to this necessity, and that steps are now being taken which may result eventually in the effectual restraint of ribboning, in the further provision of national parks, and in a path round the coasts of our island from Cape Wrath to Land's End, which shall be as free and open to walkers as our shores now are to the birds of the sea.

My acknowledgements are due to Messrs. Longmans Green & Co., to the British Academy, to Messrs. Macmillan & Co., to Charles Scribner & Sons, and to the publishers of the *Spectator*, of *John O' London's Weekly*, of the *Contemporary Review*, of the *Teacher's World*, of the *Saturday Review of Literature*, and of the *London Mercury*, for their kind permission to make use once more of material which, in the first instance, they were good enough to present to their readers.

August 1939.   H. A. L. F.

CONTENTS

I

IF NAPOLEON HAD ESCAPED TO AMERICA[1]

INVITED by my friend Sir John Squire to contribute to a volume of hypothetical history I have here advanced the thesis that Napoleon, instead of surrendering to the British after Waterloo, made good his escape to America and that a Danish ship lying off La Rochelle carried him to Boston.

This is no wild flight of fancy. Among the designs which formed themselves in Napoleon's brain during his retreat to the sea was the plan of mending his broken fortunes in the New World. There he would find many circumstances which appeared to favour the grand design of his life: the French Catholics in Quebec ill-disposed to their Protestant British Sovereign, the United States lately delivered from a bitter war with the British and exulting in the recollection of a British defeat, the Spanish Colonies of South America chafing under the yoke of their Bourbon king, and preparing under the leadership of Simon Bolivar to shake themselves free of Europe. It was no extravagant conjecture that in the Western Hemisphere the verdict of Waterloo might yet be reversed on appeal.

NEVER shall I forget that August evening. The Harvard boys were dispersed for their vacation, and had I not been expecting a box of books from France, I too should have been far away from the

[1] *If it had happened otherwise*, edited by J. C. Squire, 1931.

stifling heat of Boston, and not idly watching a foreign frigate (a Dane, they said) as she slowly worked her way up towards the quay. After the scorching heat of the day, the evening breeze on the banks of the Charles was pleasant, so I stood watching, and a thought crossed my mind, that my books might be in the hold of that ship, for I was to lecture that fall to the sophomore class on recent French literature, and was awaiting with some impatience the latest piece from Chateaubriand.

Suddenly I saw him. There could be no mistaking the figure as he stood there, with his three-cornered hat on his head, and his arms folded across his breast, looking just as in the pictures, only a little fatter and paler than I expected to see him. I bowed low, and he returned my salute. Then, as he stepped ashore, I came forward and welcomed him in French.

The power and dignity of his opening words struck me with the force of a revelation. 'Napoleon, the martyr of Liberty, the enemy of Popes and Kings, claims the hospitality of your Protestant Republic!' I replied in French that we Americans had just concluded a war with the English, who had cruelly bombarded our capital, and that he would receive a warm welcome. At this he smiled, and then proceeded with incredible rapidity to pour into me a volley of questions as to my parentage, my religion, my fortune, my calling, and many other details of my life and habits, which I answered as best I might. Meanwhile, a small company of French ladies and gentlemen had disembarked, and showing evident signs of delight at the sound of the French tongue, clasped my hand and eagerly urged me to find accommodation for the Emperor and his suite.

As you know, Napoleon's first night on American soil was spent in my uncle George's fine new, brick house in Tontine Crescent, Franklin Place.

The next day being Sunday, the Emperor must needs accompany the family to the Old South Meeting House. Indeed nothing would content him but to carry with some ostentation my uncle's Bible, which he affected to read during the greater part of the service. As we walked home, he asked me what religion was most popular in Boston. I said, 'Congregationalist'. '*Espèce de Jésuite?*' he asked. When I told him that congregationalists were convinced Huguenots, who much objected to Bishops, he nodded and said that they acted rightly, that Bishops should certainly be kept *en bride*, and that it was fortunate for Boston that the city was not under the Pope.

All through his stay in Boston, the Emperor made a point of attending the church services. '*L'Amérique vaut bien une messe,*' he would say; but since he never succeeded in learning enough English to understand a word of what was said, or even to pronounce the word Massachusetts ('*Massachusse*', he would call it), the spiritual profit which he derived from his church-going cannot have been great. What really seemed to interest him most at this time was not religion, but the history of the war with the British in Canada, which had just been concluded. He would send me to search out notable citizens who had played a part by sea or land in that conflict, and would closely interrogate them. When he learned of the deserters from the English frigates who had fought against King George, his eyes sparkled with delight. 'The English marine power is decaying,' he said. 'In the next war the islanders will be defeated at sea.'

As you may imagine, the news that the Emperor was in Boston spread through the country like wild-fire. People flocked from every quarter to see him. A special service of coaches was run from Philadelphia and New York. Crowds of newspaper men waited outside the apartments which had been reserved for his use by the State, and whenever he walked abroad, followed him with their note-books and pencils. Some of the most illustrious figures of our age, Mr. Cabot, Judge Parsons, Mr. Webster, and Mr. Mason, were anxious to shake him by the hand, and to ascertain his views on the American Constitution.

On the great day of his public reception at the State House the crowd was indescribable, stretching across State Street, and even into the common beyond. At that hour he shone with a double lustre as our latest American citizen, and as the immortal Emperor of the French. As this was my first public appearance in the character of interpreter, every word of his speech is graven on my memory. 'Citizens,' he said, 'I am a Republican. I am here to pay my tribute to the Republicans of the United States, who have valiantly thrown off the despotic yoke of perfidious Albion. That tyranny which you have broken in part of the New World, I have endeavoured to destroy in the old.

The fates which have been harsh to me have been indulgent to you. I have sustained a reverse, you have
gained a victory. But do not imagine either that my
course is run, or that your destiny is accomplished.
Great tasks lie before us, great conquests to be made,
and great empires to be overthrown in Canada, in
South America, on the far side of the Pacific Ocean.
I have come, my brothers, to offer you my brain, my
heart, and my sword.'

Here he stopped for the translation, and as the
words came through in English, the women in the
audience sobbed with emotion, the men cheered till
they were hoarse, and the whole company stood
waving their handkerchiefs for five minutes together.

Then with an intense fervour he continued,
speaking in a low, thrilling voice, which filled every
corner of the hall:

'I do not forget that you are Protestants. Have I not
read your Bible? Do I not cherish it? Does it not
accompany me wherever I voyage?' (here he took a
Bible from his pocket, and showed it to his audience).
'But, citizens, the Bible has an adversary, vigilant,
unsleeping, formidable. It is the Pope. Do not
imagine that because Protestants rule in Boston, the
power of the Pope is broken in the New World. Look
at Canada, look at Mexico, look at the vast continent
of South America. Everywhere you find the Vatican
enslaving the minds and dominating the lives of men.
In a word, citizens, your task has hardly begun. The
New World awaits a Liberator.

'Have I not imprisoned a Pope? Have I not bridled

the Bishops? Have I not granted to Protestants and Jews freedom of conscience? Men of New England, I ask you to follow me. A great destiny attends us. The Briton in the North, the Bourbon in the South, hold in subjection suffering and martyred peoples. Upon you, who have secured your own freedom by valour, Providence has devolved the duty of making Liberty triumphant throughout the American Continent. In you I behold the vanguard of the human race.

'Two hundred years ago your fathers turned their backs upon the old Europe. They could not breathe the air of tyranny. The Battle of Waterloo has been as fatal to the liberties of Europe as the Battle of Philippi was fatal to the liberties of Rome. Everywhere reaction triumphs, in Britain, in France, in Italy, in Spain. The flowers of liberty which I sowed throughout Europe have been trampled under foot. The Sacred Ark is broken. The constitutions are torn to pieces. The Goddess of Liberty veils her face. Europe is no longer the place for a free man. I turn my back upon Europe. I come to you as a missionary of Liberty. When the last chain which binds America to Europe is broken, the call of democracy will pass eastward over the waters, and once more cause the thrones to tremble.'

The immediate effect of the Emperor's speech, though lessened by the necessity of translation, was greater than I could have imagined. Women and men alike rushed forward to clasp his hand, to touch his garment. The sound of sobbing was audible through the hall. Such was the crush, that the Emperor positively fainted, and had to be conveyed back with the utmost care to my uncle's house.

The next day emotion had cooled. Peace had just been concluded with England, and no one was in the mood to reopen the quarrel. It was commonly said that Andrew Jackson was a greater general than Bonaparte, for he had whipped the British at New Orleans, while Bonaparte had been soundly beaten by the same people at Waterloo. When I told this to the Emperor, for it was my commission to collect the rumours of the town, he frowned, looked fierce and intent for a few minutes, and then snapped out, '*Bêtise incroyable!*'

You must not suppose that my life was idle. Every day I was running errands for the Emperor, collecting books and maps (especially books and maps relating to Canada and Latin America) and bringing important men to see him, arranging for a series of communications with friends in New York, with Red Indian leaders, with Catholic priests in Quebec. The Emperor at this time rarely went abroad, but was busy with his books, his interviews, his dictation. Though much of his thought was hidden, it was clear that the main part of it revolved round the idea of evicting the British from Canada. One evening in mid October he sent me out to bespeak three places in the New York coach. Of his design neither I nor General Bertrand, who was selected as one of the three, were acquainted. I only noticed that, though the weather was beautifully mild, and warm as June in northern

Europe, he wore the heavy greatcoat which was spread upon his bed at night. During the journey, which lasted three days, he was at times drowsy, while at other times he would cross-question his fellow-travellers, particularly such as had any knowledge of the Canadian frontier. But it was only the second day after our arrival that I learned the true mystery of the visit and of the heavy greatcoat. There was in New York a Dutch jeweller, who had connexions with the diamond merchants in Amsterdam. How the Emperor had heard of him I do not know; but I suspect that his retentive memory had stored up this name and this address many years before, when passing through Holland, or from some paper in the possession of his brother Louis. Anyhow, Van Byl, for such was the little man's name, seemed to expect him, and showed no surprise when the Emperor, ripping up the lining of his coat, took out fifty diamonds of the best quality, and laid them on the counter. People have often wondered whence the Emperor obtained the where-withal to support his establishment; but I can say with truth that, though many of his American ad-mirers subscribed to his coffers, and he became, especially after his reception by Mr. Jefferson, the recipient of legacies, the nucleus of his fund was obtained from the sale of these stones.

From New York we proceeded up the Hudson to Albany. How can I forget the enchantment of that journey, the red and gold of the maples, the noble spread of waters, the graceful mountain outlines against the pale blue October sky, the stillness of those windless hours? Everything in the atmosphere invited to repose. Even the Emperor would sometimes surrender himself to the sweet spirit of the season, recounting ghost stories or his own adventures or lapsing into some dreamy monologue on the soul and immortality or the destiny of the Universe. Only once I remember that he spoke openly of politics. We were nearing Albany, where it was arranged that we should disembark, and have our interview with the French plotters and Indian chiefs, who had undertaken to render help during the summer expedition to Quebec. Our small steamer was moored for the night. The crew had gone to their rest. The moon was shining so brightly that one could easily read the map which the Emperor held outstretched upon his knees.

'Do you ever have presentiments?' he said to General Bertrand.

'No, Sire.'

'Look at this map. Here are the British in Canada, here are the French. You, Bertrand, will meet the Jesuit Father at M. Lemoine's in Albany. You will be conducted by him to Quebec. He will introduce you to the French notables of the province. You will speak, of course, of my care of the Mother Church. You will tell him how I restored the churches, how I made the Concordat, how the Pope came to Paris to crown me Emperor, and you will tell them that I am at hand to free a nation of French Catholics from the tyrannous yoke of a Protestant alien. You will tell them all this, *mon cher*, you will conspire with them, you will travel everywhere, laying the foundations of a great rebellion; and next spring you will return to me, and if the news be favourable, we shall march. Shall we succeed? Shall we plant the tricolour on the citadel of Quebec? Here I admit, my friends, that I have a presentiment of misfortune. The snow is unfriendly to my genius. Ah! those terrible snows in Russia!' Here he drew his coat round him and shivered. 'The British, they are nothing—but the snows! We must not allow ourselves to be caught in the snows of Canada. Sometimes I ask myself whether Canada is worth the effort. Moscow, the Kremlin, the road to India! There was glory. But a little *bicoque* like Quebec, won from a bad French general by a single volley, it is hardly worth the candle. What is the glory of conquering a frozen waste without monuments or history, bare as yon moon, but without its beauty? No, *mes amis*, let us leave the English to starve and shiver in the wilderness. Nevertheless, if our good Bertrand can add to their discomforts, we shall not regret it, *hein?*'

For the most part of his sojourn in Albany, the Emperor was closeted with French Canadians and Indian chiefs, and since a good Jesuit interpreter was available, I was sent abroad to collect the opinions of Albany and the neighbourhood as to the prospects of a new war with England. When I rejoined the Emperor, he was alone. A few hours before, the general had set out on his errand, disguised as a Jesuit Father, and charged with letters and proclamations to the Canadian French. 'Our good Bertrand is no theologian,' observed the Emperor, with a pleasant smile, 'I have been teaching him the Paternoster.'

It is not true, as some have alleged, that the capture of General Bertrand by a Canadian patrol, followed as it was by the publication of the Emperor's secret correspondence with the fathers of Laval, was the determining cause for our removal to Philadelphia. My belief is, that in any case my master had resolved to spend the winter months in the first city of the Republic, where he might meet the leading men of the time and enjoy an atmosphere more liberal than that of Puritan Boston, and that in making this decision he was confirmed by the evidence which he had received, more especially in New York, of the aversion of the leading Americans for a renewal of the war with Great Britain. Be this as it may, the confluence of Philadelphians attending the arrival of the New York coach on that third Friday in November was, in spite of the intercepted documents, most astounding. One could hardly believe that a population, of which the Quakers formed so large an element, should, thus soon, have passed the sponge of oblivion over the Emperor's recent professions of faith in the Roman Church. But curiosity is mightier than religion. A general returning from a triumphant campaign could not have been greeted with more enthusiasm. Men and women pressed forward to shake his hand, to pat him on the back, to chaff him with the utmost good nature on Bertrand's mishap. The Emperor did not take kindly to these homely demonstrations. From the first he seemed to bear a grudge against the Philadelphians, which was deepened by two untoward circumstances, their admiration for Lafayette, and the praises of General Andrew Jackson, which entered into every conversation. 'I guess our Andrew licks creation,' they would say, at which my master would turn on his heel hissing out '*Imbéciles*', and bitterly annoyed at so lax a judgement.

There was one very painful scene. It was on the occasion of his public reception in Independence Hall (as we must now call the State House) when in the presence of Mr. and Mrs. Madison, Mr. Calhoun, and other eminent men, he completely lost his self-control at the close of the last of a long series of eloquent speeches, all nominally framed to do him honour, but nevertheless chiefly concerned with the excellence of American institutions, and the brilliant strategy of the popular general, who had recently whipped the British at New Orleans. 'You compare your Jackson to Napoleon,' he burst out, 'you do not know what war is. There is more genius in my little finger than in the whole body of your General Jackson. I tell you, Jackson is a mediocre general. If Jackson had a thousand men, and I had fifty, I tell you that I would beat Jackson ten times in eleven.' I was naturally too discreet to translate this passage literally, and as the special friends of General Jackson were unacquainted with French, the incident passed without serious consequences.

From that moment I noticed that Napoleon's thoughts turned steadily southwards and westwards. The winter climate of Philadelphia, which was colder than he expected, may have had something to do with this, but more serious was his antipathy to the nature of the North American people. He would say that North America had all the faults of England, and none of its advantages. He complained of the language, so clumsy, obscure, ill sounding; of the religion, so tedious; of the moral standards, so severe that he could not even stroll abroad with Madame Walewska (who had arrived unexpectedly on November 29), of the absence of a court and an aristocracy, of the easy-going familiarity of our ways, of our whisky, our tobacco, of the common habit of expectoration, and of our rough, uneven roads.

I fancy that in a society devoid of social deference and speaking a language which he could not comprehend, he felt that he had no great role to play. 'They compliment me as if I were a god,' he complained bitterly, 'but they treat me as an equal. They do not even see the difference between the victor of Marengo and Austerlitz, and a vain coxcomb like Lafayette, who could not control the Paris *canaille*.'

More and more he thought of the South, of establishing perhaps a little kingdom in Louisiana, where French was spoken, and the climate was warm, and of thence effecting the liberation of South America. 'It was a mistake to sell Louisiana to the Americans,' he said more than once. 'But *n'importe*, they will see in me one of the historic glories of France. Who will think of the miserable Jackson, when Napoleon appears to claim the allegiance of a French people?' It was at this period that he wrote a letter to his brother Joseph urging him to come to New Orleans in the following spring, with such money and supplies as he could collect.

The visit of the two Spaniards, which was destined to have so great an influence on the history of the world, was kept a great secret. Even the Philadelphia news-men never got an inkling of the fact that late every night during the last week of November the agents of Bolivar were closeted with the Emperor. Even I was not admitted to these conferences, but I could guess what was a-foot from the maps and books, which I was commanded to buy, and from the way in which, from that moment onwards, the Emperor's mind seemed to be occupied by South American affairs to the exclusion of other interests.

It is idle to pretend that the arrival of Madame Walewska and her little child was not an embarrassment to the Emperor and his suite. Nothing could have been more unfortunately timed. Just when it was important that the Emperor's mind should be concentrated on his great design, this beautiful woman, to whom he was deeply attached, came to distract him with her passionate attentions. In Philadelphia, where everything is immediately known, her arrival could not be concealed. The newspapers were full of the mystery of Citizen Bonaparte's Polish lady friend. The Quakers came in a deputation to protest. Only the dressmakers were really pleased, and for many years contrived to attire the belles of Philadelphia after the fashion of the Polish beauty. Fortunately time adjusts all things. When Mrs. Madison, in her

blue velvet gown and plumes, had called at Spruce
Street, followed by that famous wit and leader of
bon ton, the Abbé Correa, the tempest of criticism
subsided, and the adventuress of yesterday was an-
nounced to be an excellent little woman, and much
maligned.

Not a fortnight later there followed a visit so strange
and important that every detail of it, even after this
distance of years, is stamped upon my mind. I can
see the Emperor sitting in his shirt-sleeves, for the
heat of the stove, and lifting his eyes from a Spanish
news-sheet, as I came to announce that two English
visitors were below. I remember his first dark suspicions, exchanged so swiftly for the brightest hopes,
when I had ascertained that our visitors were none
other than the famous Lady Holland and Dr. Allen,
her secretary; how he sprang to his feet crying,
'Lady Holland here! This may be the crisis of our
fortunes. Tell her to wait a few moments, and
return to me.'

The Emperor had determined to receive the great
English lady *en grande tenue*. As he dressed, he con-
versed rapidly.

'I remember Lady Holland. She came to me at Mal-
maison during the peace. Does she keep her looks?
She must be fifty. Is it possible to amuse oneself with
Lady Holland? No? She has a great soul, I am sure
of that. Were I to marry Lady Holland, the English
Whigs would follow me, and I could dethrone George.
You say that her husband still lives, but he is doubt-
less old as well as gouty. Bah! What does it matter?

A woman who crosses the Atlantic to pay her respects to a man is his in advance!'

I said I thought it unlikely that Lady Holland would divorce a husband to whom she was attached.

'You do not understand Lady Holland,' he replied warmly. 'She has a great soul. We shall comprehend one another. In the new world, polygamy should be tolerated. I believe that if I had reigned longer, I should have induced the Pope to tolerate polygamy in the Sugar Islands. Lady Holland will understand this point of view, she will be my interpreter, my ally, perhaps even a wife, who knows?' Then drawing himself up, and buttoning the last button of his uniform, 'Lady Holland will follow her star. She will inscribe her name on the annals of history as the companion of Napoleon.'

I observed that while Lady Holland admired the Emperor as a statesman and a general, she was not likely, at her age, to fall in love. The English were always cold. 'You will see,' replied the Emperor, laying his finger on his nose. 'Lady Holland will prove the exception to the rule.'

With that he bade me show Lady Holland into the room, but on no account the English secretary. 'Engage Dr. Allen downstairs,' he added. 'Interrogate him. Find out the total (*global*) fortune of Lord Holland, how much of it is in land, how much in houses, how much in stocks and shares, how much Lady Holland has brought with her. Ask the same questions with respect to Allen's estate. It is not only English lords who are rich. Fox was not a lord, but he could spend money. Perhaps it was not his own. That is likely.' Here he paused, as if in meditation. Then, as I was leaving the room, he added, 'Do not forget to inquire whether they know any rich Americans.'

I confess that I found it impossible to execute these instructions. Dr. Allen, who appeared to be a learned man, spoke of the historical antiquities of Massachusetts, asking me many questions, which I was unable to answer. It was therefore a relief when, an hour later, I heard the Emperor's bell. As I entered the *cabinet de travail*, Lady Holland was making a low reverence. 'Madam, we will regenerate the world together,' said my master sublimely as she kissed his hand.

Overcome with emotion, the lady rejoined her friend and drove away.

'What did you make of the secretary?' asked the Emperor. I said that he was a learned man, who had travelled in Spain, and was interested in antiquities.

'Well, that is better than nothing. We shall want antiquarians. I took antiquarians with me to Egypt. They shall accompany me to South America. Allen can be better employed with the glorious monuments of the Incas than with the mouldy relics of his damp little island. I know the history of England. It is nothing. But South America! A vast continent, untouched by the spade, rich with extinct and brilliant civilizations! What a noble field for the savant! Our expedition will infuse new life into South America. It will do more. It will regenerate Allen!' Here he laughed till his sides shook. 'And stay, there is another use for Allen. We will make him a lord. Then he will marry one of these rich Boston ladies. Lord Allen will sound very well. You see, *mon cher* (rubbing his hands), fortune opens out on every side. What does it matter to the Universe if Allen is a lord! It is a name only, but if it brings us the *dot* of Allen's ugly American wife—that is worth while, I think.

'As for Miladi, she does not resemble Walewska. They would be antipathetic. See to it, Claude, that these ladies do not meet. Miladi is an *esprit fort*. She reasons like a man. I call her an English Madame de Staël, but better looking, and not so unreasonable. Yes, Lady Holland is decidedly more intelligent than Madame de Staël. ᚦut bah! how ridiculous intelligent women are!

'Still, we must humour Lady Holland. In Philadelphia, perhaps, where the English are not popular, she will be suspect; but one never knows. Lady Holland is a *grande dame*. We will employ her to relieve the rich Quakers of some of their superfluities.'

Lady Holland's arrival was as helpful as the appearance of Madame Walewska had been otherwise. For it appeared that this proud and beautiful English lady (much as she despised the North Americans) was as eager to spill English blood in the liberation of South America as the Emperor himself, and that she had even met Miranda on the occasion of his visit to London. Need I picture my master's delight in finding that the leading Whigs in England were all Spanish 'Liberales!' For the better part of a fortnight he could

think of little but the assistance which might be drawn
from English Whigs to the furtherance of his great
designs. One day he even appeared at *déjeuner* wearing Whig favours. '*N'est-ce pas que je suis Vig, Miladi?
Fox même n'était plus foncièrement Vig que moi.*' I have
never known him more cheerful. He counted that with
the wife of Lord Holland, and the Whigs, all the dis-
banded idle soldiers and sailors of England could be
enticed over to share the great adventure of liberating
South America. In a letter addressed to a prominent
Philadelphian Quaker he spoke of the power of Spain
in South America as the great obstacle to a Pan-
American peace, but to Lady Holland he said, not
altogether in jest, 'You English are a race of bandits.
You must not forget your traditions. Regard me as
one who combines the qualities of a Raleigh and a
Fox.'

The situation in South America, as we came to
learn, was at that time critical. The Republican revolt,
which for the past four years had blazed and splut-
tered all over the Continent, now seemed almost
extinguished save in the Plate province. Morillo's
royalist forces had stamped out the rebellion in Venezuela and in Granada. Bolivar was a fugitive. A
bloodthirsty reaction was running its evil course from
one end of the Continent to another.

The night before Lady Holland sailed for Europe,
Napoleon divulged to me the broad outline of his
plans. He would first go to Washington to press upon
the Government the conquest of Florida. 'Jackson is
a bad general, but he is capable of commanding the

army of Florida!' Then he would proceed to New
Orleans, where he had already made an assignation
with two great leaders of the South American revolt,
Bolivar and Sucre.

'At New Orleans,' he observed, 'I shall feel at home.
My Latins will be about me. It is there that I shall
organize the conquest of South America.'

'Sire,' observed Las Casas, 'it is an immense project,
greater and more difficult than the conquest of Russia.
They tell me that in those swamps and forests of
Venezuela the yellow fever is worse than it was in
San Domingo.'

'You do not understand the war of the future. How
does one tame a land, rich beyond dreams, but in-
habited by a sprinkling of half-starved, superstitious,
quarrelsome Creoles? You think that I do not understand the Creole nature?' Here he paused, and we
remembered that Empress Josephine was a Creole.
'I tell you that Creoles are not like Prussians. It is
not by force that Creoles are ruled, but by seduction
and gold. Besides in this new world the art of war
takes on a wider aspect. Arms alone do not suffice.
Empires will be won by propaganda and gold, by
men of affairs and architects and savants. Byron will
write odes which we will translate and scatter everywhere, in Caracas, in Bogota, in Lima. At New Orleans
we will set up a great bureau of literature, which will
inundate the Continent. The Quaker mission is organized. Lady Holland's mad admiral has sworn to
help us. A young French soldier named de Vigny
raises a legion from among my veterans. The English

adventurers, Whigs, brigands, old soldiers, sailors escaping the Pressgang, will flock to my standard. The *rendez-vous* is arranged. It is Margarita, a small island in the Caribbean Sea. We will hurl our English on Morillo. Ah! *mon Dieu!* Make no mistake. The yellow fever will not leave the English unvisited, nor the royalists either.'

By this time the Emperor, having emptied his own snuff-box, seized mine without a word of apology, took a pinch, and pocketed the box.

'We shall take the money of the Quakers, *bien entendu*, but we shall not deceive them, for we shall give to South America a lasting peace.'

The story of Napoleon's visit to Mr. Jefferson at Monticello is well known. It has furnished the theme of so many pictures (all the world knows Sully's fifty thousand dollar canvas) and descriptive essays that I would not mention it but for one circumstance. After that visit we had no more criticism of Napoleon as the Attila of his age, the blood-thirsty tyrant, the enemy of the human race. It was sufficient for the citizens of our country that the immortal Mr. Jefferson, the chief author of the Declaration of Independence, had received him in his beautiful home, shown him the library, the garden, and the mills of Monticello, and that he should have been there entertained for six days as an honoured guest. Hour after hour did Napoleon converse with that venerable and famous friend of human liberty, speaking of the far-reaching plans for the regeneration of Europe, which had been foiled at Waterloo, of his friendship with the English Whigs, and of his desire to see South America freed by the joint efforts of the patrons of liberty in Britain, in France, and in the United States. My belief is that Mr. Jefferson, who at this time was anxious to be cordial with England, was originally persuaded to relent towards Napoleon by the news of Lady Holland's visit, and that our invitation to Monticello was due to that cause. However this may be, there can be no doubt that Mr. Jefferson felt the fascination of his guest. For often afterwards he spoke of him with enthusiasm, as a friend of Liberty and humane letters, in whom all that was generous and addicted to virtue in the Anglo-Saxon people might find a prop and support.

It is largely to Mr. Jefferson's influence with the Government at Washington that, despite many representations from the envoys of Britain and France, Napoleon was permitted to establish in New Orleans a centre of political activity, so intense as to convulse the fortunes of a continent. Never, save perhaps during the first years of the consulate, were his energies so happily inspired. There were indeed days when a certain languor seemed to overtake him; but these would be followed by a sudden recovery of nervous power, which enabled him to accomplish in a day what an ordinary mortal could scarcely hope to achieve in a month.

When I think what was accomplished in those wonderful eighteen months—the gathering of the army of Venezuela, of the army of Granada, the raising of the African volunteer corps from the southern plantations, the defeat of Morillo's royalists by the combined levies of Bolivar and Sucre on a plan of campaign devised by the Emperor at Port-au-Prince, the bribing of Peru, the great workshops of republican propaganda established in Bogota and Lima, I am lost in amazement at the amount which was accomplished in so small a time. It is no exaggeration to say that in these eighteen months the foundations were laid for the South American Republic.

I can see him, even at this distance of time, in his broad panama hat, reviewing the black troops upon his vast plantations, for you must know that a torrent of legacies had suddenly made him the largest slave owner in the Southern States. I can see him leading the cotillion with Madame Walewska, he so grave, she so radiant, in one of those warm, perfumed, southern nights, when the light of the moon and stars seems to outshine the yellow lamps. I can see him in his *cabinet de travail* in the Cabildo (which had been placed at his disposal by the City) dictating to three secretaries at once, in his quick, nervous, jerky voice, or lying on the floor sticking pins into maps, or again, as in moments of relaxation, he held us all spellbound by his anecdotes and recollections. I remember, too, the day on which he received the news that the Pope (influenced, it was said, by a Polish Cardinal) had annulled his marriage with Marie Louise. All that is long ago now, but I remember it as if it were yesterday, the black gloom of the Emperor, his cherished son being now declared illegitimate, the triumphant joy of the Polish lady, and the eager preparations which were made in the town for a popular wedding.

As you know, it turned out otherwise. When the Emperor started upon his great expedition on the last day of August 1817, Madame Walewska, having hardly recovered from the birth of her second son, was left behind. To cross the sea, and then to undertake a journey on mule-back through swamps and forests, and across the lofty Andes to Lima was no work for a delicate woman. Do not, however, suppose that my master was heartless. He grieved at the parting, and it was only after he had reached Lima, the ancient capital of Pizarro, and there discovered how high and proud was the tone of the Spanish aristocracy, that he determined to marry the Montemira girl.

Little satisfaction did he obtain from a union founded upon hard political calculation, for the girl was as cold as ice and stiff as starch, her blood soured by priestcraft, and her father, the marquis, a parched old mummy, who thought of nothing in the world but his descent from the Inca Princes.

Mr. Bancroft and Mr. Prescott have both employed their famous pens on a description of Napoleon's journey from Caracas to Lima—the long line of mules, litters, *valencins*, and carts, the African bodyguard, the light horsemen, Spanish, American, English, French (these in small numbers) and North Americans, the body of picked American savants and architects, the corps of French veterans, the three hundred deserters from English ships, the three theatrical companies,

English, French, and Spanish, the musicians, the numerous printing-presses which passed over the country which had already been cleared of enemy forces by the armies of Bolivar and Sucre. Such a triumphal procession South America had never seen. Long before the liberator had reached Lima, he was master of every South American heart. Even the forces of nature were defied, for who has not heard of *Le Cid*, played on a sunny afternoon in a sheltered cup of the towering Andes?

In Peru he found that spirit of social deference, the lack of which had constantly pained him in the North; but notwithstanding it was easy to see that he was restless and unhappy. There was something huge and unearthly about the landscape which haunted him. 'This', he said, 'is a country of vast mountains and small minds. There is more life in a village of Provence than in the whole province of Peru.' Startling as his triumph had been—for could anything be more wonderful than the creation in so short a time of a federal Republic of South America?—he was still hungry. To rule Creoles and South American Indians in that damp shadowland seemed an unworthy conclusion to a great career.

Yet Mr. Bancroft, in describing his work in South America, does not hesitate to compare it to the achievements of George Washington and Alexander Hamilton, the first supreme in war, the second the architect of the glorious American constitution; but I have heard that the great and good Mr. Jefferson in the closing year of his life expressed his disappointment in Napoleon, saying that the South American Federation, though in name a Republic, was in fact little better than a military tyranny, and that the governors of the provinces, Bolivar, Sucre, San Martin, and the rest, were no friends to democratic liberty, but tyrants supported by Pretorian guards. Candour compels me to admit that the venerable statesman has, with his habitual perspicacity, divined a truth which long escaped the notice of the North American people.

Indeed, if the exact truth must be told, he never esteemed at their full value our noble institutions. 'The *Clermont*, that little steam packet on the Hudson,' he would say, 'is worth more than all your Jeffersons and Madisons. With steam you Americans will revolutionize the world. Distance will be vanquished. Who knows but if some day great American armies may not be conveyed across the Atlantic Ocean, and mould the destinies of Europe? But your constitution! It is the worst in the world, the fabric of idealogues living in a Utopia of bucolic dreams. What great enterprise can your President achieve in four years?'

I reminded him that in less than four years he had reconstructed France.

'Ah!' he said, 'but then I did not allow myself to be hampered by politicians. Everything in France, the army, the foreign policy, the police, the education, the taxes, was under my hands. Your President cannot make a treaty without the Senate, or raise a dollar without the House of Representatives. In England such institutions may succeed, for England is governed by an experienced aristocracy; but in this country, where one man is as good as another, there must be a supreme figure to stir the flame of admiration and make the wheels of history go round.'

On the first evening of his arrival at the plantations which had been left him under the will of the beautiful Comtesse de Morainville, he recurred to the subject of the destiny of North America, saying that although he was now a wealthy proprietor in Louisiana with slaves and sugar-cane, not to speak of a fine cellar of good old Madeira, he would never tolerate the life of a planter. We were sitting on the porch, sipping lemonade and fingering our ices. The great yellow river flowed behind the orange groves. It was that delicious hour before the swift coming on of a southern night. Monsieur de Vigny, a young soldier and man of letters (who had recently arrived with General Foy from France), spoke with poetic enchantment of the beauty of the great river and the evening sky, and of the delights offered by an existence spent among these soft and tranquil scenes.

My master did not scruple to interrupt his flow. 'Ah! our young friend is a poet. It is not by poetry that the Americans grow sugar and cotton, but by a stout whip of cow-hide applied to the backs of their African slaves. Jefferson is an idealogue, but I observed that neither in his home nor on his property did he dispense with the services of these useful creatures. As for me, I am no idealogue like Jefferson, but wealth does not interest me as an end. What is the value of ownership? But power, glory, the foundation of institutions, these are the ambitions of a lofty soul. You will see that all the wealth which I have gathered in this country will be employed towards great ends.'

General Foy then asked whether the vast expanse of North America did not hold out fine prospects for the ambitious man.

'For the traveller, the discoverer, the seeker after wealth, yes. Not so for the statesman or the soldier. America is not a state, but a company of exploitation. The policy of Providence is to sprinkle this continent with individuals. The function of the statesman is to manœuvre with masses. I tell you that the North American does not understand politics, and has no need of politics. He wants to get rich, and he is right. To develop the resources of this continent by mining, farming, manufacturing, that is his destiny, but it is not a fate which I desire to share.'

The world has never ceased to wonder why in the midst of the pleasures and glories of his Peruvian home, while he was the undisputed master of a continent, and the dictator of innumerable schemes for its social and intellectual advancement (a handsome new quarter designed by Mr. Bulfinch, principally for the accommodation of the French veterans, had just been added to the city of Pizarro), he took the astonishing resolution which led to his end. If he had retired to a monastery, like Charles V, it would have seemed to his Spanish-speaking subjects more intelligible than the course which he adopted. The theory of Dr. Springmann, that it was a case of *tædium vitæ*, I dismiss at once. Nor do I agree with those French historians who assign the blame to his high-born Spanish wife, for if the truth be told, he found among the Creoles of the *Calle del peligro* many sources of consolation for that insipid lady. My theory is that a hidden spring of memory was touched by the news, coming to him in the autumn of 1818, that some Indian peoples had risen against the English, and that an invitation from the Peshwa, reaching him at the very moment when he was dictating his Egyptian memories, lit a certain flame in his mind, which grew and grew until it burnt its way through every obstacle.

A few words which he spoke late one night in the Palace garden confirm me in this opinion. 'Great men', he said, 'speak in prophecy. After all, Columbus was right. The way to the Indies is by the West.' Then, twitching me by the ear, he continued, 'Do you know that Wellington made his first campaigns in India? Perhaps it is fated that, where Wellington began, there I should end. Who knows? I say to you, India is the Achilles' heel of English power. Already the proud islanders tremble for their plunder. The Indians murmur. They await a man. Something whispers to my heart that the Battle of Waterloo will be avenged on the plains of Bengal.'

It is now established beyond doubt that the *Galvanino* went down with all hands in that great November gale off the coast of Java. Of the voyage nothing is known, and of the preparations for the voyage very little certainly to me. By what arts Napoleon induced the commander of that Chilean vessel to convey him across the Pacific I have never learnt, for the whole secret was so skilfully kept that even I, the confidential secretary and interpreter, never divined the purpose of Admiral Blanco's nightly visits to the Palace. All I know is that on the morning of September 23 it was found that Napoleon had sailed from Callao, on an unknown errand, with fifteen of his old companions in arms, and a crew of deserters from the English Navy, and that the ex-King Joseph was governing the Republic in his place. Mr. Prescott's fine phrase, 'A South American Charlemagne,' must not be pressed too far. It is true that Napoleon's travelling inspectorate (save for the fact that it was everywhere attended by a train of light artillery) was avowedly modelled on the *Missi dominici* of the Frankish Empire; but 'the Friends of Liberty', a club or faction of the Emperor's South American adherents, highly organized, alone entitled to bear arms, and alone privileged to vote at elections, recalled the party groups of medieval Italy; while other features of the South American Constitution, such as the division of the settled districts into departments and the curtailment of the Legislative sessions to a period of fourteen days, were clearly derived from Imperial France.

Such institutions Mr. Jefferson was justified in regarding as falling short of the spirit and intention of his immortal Declaration of Independence, and their acceptance only to be explained by the exhaustion bred of five years' civil war, from which the South American people were then suffering.

My belief is that the Emperor (for so I continue to think of him) held the South American population in deep contempt. Save for Generals Sucre and San Martin, no leaders of the revolution inspired him with confidence. In Bolivar he beheld the flame of genius, but too often obscured by the hateful fumes of animal passion. 'Some day', he would say, 'I shall be compelled to execute that creature. Otherwise he will shock the world with his lusts and atrocities.' In a word, he held that South America was not fit for liberty, and were it not for the curb of strong institutions, would lapse into a century of chaos. This, however, was not the language which he used in public. To the world at large he spoke of 'our provisional institutions', and hinted that great preparations were being made for a golden age of Liberty. That my master was insincere, I am reluctant to believe. Honesty, however, compels me to admit that the diligent researches of Mr. Bancroft and Mr. Prescott among the Archives of Lima have failed to discover any trace of these preparations.

Of the twenty-eight false Napoleons who appeared in the United States during President Munroe's administration, three were women, claiming to have changed souls with the Emperor. Of these, Ellen Jane Mason, of Roxbury, Mass., was the most successful, for despite the failure of her costly action at law for the possession of the Louisiana plantations, she left a fortune of one hundred thousand dollars made by this deception.

II

BIMILLENARIES[1]

I. VIRGIL

(Oct. 15, 1930)

WE are met here to-day on the Ides of October (*Octobres Maro consecravit Idus*) to celebrate the bimillenary of Virgil's birth, with a lecture by the President of Magdalen on 'Virgil in English Poetry'. The history of literary taste is for the most part a tissue of rapid changes, the renown and popularity of authors waxing and waning like the moon. But the fame of Virgil is a fixed star, shining in the firmament with a steady light. His supremacy in Latin letters, which was acknowledged in his short lifetime, has never been challenged, not even in the generation which was captivated by the African exuberance of Apulaeus, or during the darkest ages of medieval ignorance, when he was accorded a superstitious homage as a prophet or wizard. So the influence of this shy poet, nature-lover, scholar, savant, patriot, so delicate in taste, so grave, precise, and well balanced in mind, so full of romance and vision and pathos, has been for nearly two thousand years a force in European civilization, working always against vulgarity and the uninspired view of human fate. Students drawn from every intellectual quarter have found in Virgil an answer to their needs. To the Roman citizen he brought the gospel of Empire, and

[1] A Five-minutes' Broadcast from the British Academy.

of duty, to the medieval Christian intimations of the
Messiah and of the association of the Christian Faith
with the Roman polity. Among Latin Grammarians
his authority was such that, were his works to disappear, they could be recovered almost completely
from the citations of the pedants. Rhetoricians found
in him models of eloquence, ritualists a mine of
sacerdotal lore. In every civilized land the young have
been harnessed to his exacting chariot. Yet neither
the lapse of time nor the unremitting labour of the
schools weakens the hold of the poet who inspired
Dante and Petrarch, and gave to the Middle Ages in
the beautiful story of Dido a favourite heroine of
romance. It is perhaps some indication of the sustained perfection of his greatest work that there are
no two books of the *Aeneid* universally judged to be
the best. If the popular favourites are the fourth and
sixth, Mr. Gladstone preferred the second, Mon-
taigne the fifth, and Sainte-Beuve the eighth.

Had Virgil been merely a patriotic Italian poet,
'laying the spoils of Homer on the steps of the Capitol',
we should not be here to-day; but Virgil's patriotism
was no narrow and exclusive thing. He saw in the rise
of the Roman Empire a new hope for the human race,
a hope of peace, of order, of civilization. The view
which he preached was long dominant in Europe.
Dante, writing in the spirit of the great concluding
passage of the first *Georgic*, assigns Brutus and Cassius,
the murderers of Julius Caesar, to the lowest pit of
the Inferno with Judas Iscariot, the betrayer of Christ.
As Empire and Papacy were the twin lights of the

world, so the foes of Empire were the friends of darkness and chaos. The taste for Imperialism comes and goes, but Virgil's message transcends all politics, and when the fabric of civilization is threatened by the tremors of anarchy and war, his grave music floats above the tumult with its strains of piety, of mansuetude, and of hope like the inner voice of humanity itself.

II. AUGUSTUS CAESAR[1]
(63 B.C.—A.D. 1937)

NOT alone does Italy celebrate the bimillenary of Augustus. From distant Canada an ever-wakeful eye notes the solemn occasion, an ever-moving pen indites the appropriate tribute. John Buchan, a familiar name, throwing off the sepulchral integuments of an English peerage, comes forward once more, despite the heavy charge of his proconsulate, with yet another admirable historical biography. His Augustus, a task begun many years since, and completed in the leisure of two Canadian winters, is a sequel to the earlier volume on Julius Caesar, but covers more difficult and intricate ground, for the materials, though lately enlarged by epigraphical and archaeological discovery, are still very scanty, and the field of conjecture is proportionately large. The Governor-General of Canada has, however, shirked no labour. His wise, eloquent, and sensitive pages everywhere bear traces of a scholar's scrupulous diligence. Augustus may have

[1] *Augustus*, by John Buchan (Hodder & Stoughton. 21s.). Reprinted from *The Spectator*, Oct. 29, 1937.

been the least romantic of great men, but the master builder of the imperial polity of Rome deserves a good biography and has got it.

It was characteristic of Mommsen that he should have ended his great history of Rome with Julius Caesar the soldier, and should have seen in him the true founder of the Roman Empire. Yet it. is to Augustus rather than to Julius, to the man of peace rather than to the man of war, that the permanence of the imperial fabric is really due. Augustus indeed was no stranger to war. 'At the age of nineteen years,' he writes, 'on my own authority and at my own cost, I raised an army by means of which I liberated the Republic from the oppression of a tyrannical faction'; but his great title to fame rests upon the fact that he secured for the civilized world two centuries of peace.

Every quality of civilian excellence, 'iron self-command, infinite patience, and infallible judgement of facts and men', in a word that 'profound practical intelligence which is far rarer in history than a seminal idealism', are justly attributed to this wonderful figure. If, like all great men, Augustus had a sense of mission, he had little of mysticism. A banking stock is not productive of this peculiar spiritual fruit, and it was not for nothing that Augustus came from a family of bankers. If, then, his bequest to Rome was, as Lord Tweedsmuir so well describes it, 'one of the most complex yet smooth-running systems of government known in history, a government "at once expert and professional",' this was not because Augustus had formed any preconceived idea of how a great human society should be ruled, but because as each successive emergency bore down upon him he met it with instinctive tact and a sense for the most prudent, which was sometimes also the boldest, solution. A man of peace and temperamentally disposed to clemency, he yet did not shrink on occasions from stern and cruel action. He sanctioned, albeit with hesitation, the savage proscriptions of 43 B.C. which resulted in the death of Cicero. He slew the two sons of Cleopatra and exiled his daughter and granddaughter, but the distinguishing note of his government was always a paternal benevolence, his ideal a well-conducted, harmonious society, based upon wholesome family life; his creed the religion of Numa, 'a religion of usage and sentiment' rather than of doctrine. His prescription for government was a judicious blend of old and new things, of the tribunician power and proconsular authority, of the popular and autocratic, of republican office and hellenistic monarchy.

He was wise in the choice of his friends and helpers; in Agrippa, first soldier of the Empire, who won his victories; in Maecenas, 'the adroit and subtle minister of propaganda', who brought the men of letters on to his side; in Ateius Capito, the great lawyer; and fortunate also in the beautiful Livia, who was for fifty-two years the married partner of his life, and whose character is now effectually cleared from the foul aspersions of the gossip-writers. Above all he was fortunate in his length of days, for his was a task which, like all the great things of life, required time as a

condition of achievement. Yet dark shadows and disappointments also awaited him. He had no son. His
two favourite grandsons died in early manhood. The
third, though commended by Lord Tweedsmuir as a
keen fisherman—'and few anglers', he adds, 'are altogether vile'—finished his life in exile and was probably
half an idiot. The early death of Marcellus, a cherished
nephew, shattered many bright hopes, and inspired
the noble lament which is one of the most famous
passages in the Sixth book of Virgil's *Aeneid*. Two
stepsons were able soldiers, but of these Drusus
perished in Germany, a great loss to the Empire, for
he was a man of fine and human quality; so that in the
end Tiberius alone, 'proud, awkward, unconciliatory'
was left to inherit the purple.

That Augustus possessed supreme advantages is
certain, and the source of the confidence which
marked his steps. Heir to the illustrious Julius, he
was so wealthy, for in addition to his family fortune,
which was considerable, he could call upon the
treasures of Egypt, that he was able to lighten the
public burdens and relieve unemployment without
recourse to new taxation. No formidable competitor
stood in his path. He was assailed by no militant or
powerful creed. His ascent to power came at a time
when all classes longed for those very blessings of
peace and security which it was in his nature and
capacity to provide. That his interpretation of auto-
cracy was subtler than that of Julius was no cause of
offence to the Caesarians. They were content that
their hero was avenged, and were not concerned with

the degree to which his dreams and visions were trans-
muted in the fabric of the Augustan structure.

The name Augustus was a term of honour, not a
title of office. Lord Tweedsmuir suggests that it was
probably the idea of Maecenas, the *éminence grise* in
the background. 'Its plain meaning', he writes, 'was
much that of the words "by the Grace of God"; it
suggested a favourite of Heaven; some one, in Dio's
words, "more than human," but at the same time a
man and no eastern divinity', and this title, like that
other title of Princeps, or leader, adopted by the great
nephew of Caesar, was in harmony with that policy of
polite and politic fiction which is a distinctive feature
of the Augustan structure. When the emergency
powers which had helped the leader to save society
were solemnly handed back to the people, they were in
fact resumed in other forms. Augustus has described
his view of the position. 'I declined', he writes, 'to accept any office inconsistent with the institutions of our
ancestors. I stood before all others in authority, but
of actual power I possessed no more than my colleagues in each separate magistracy.'

The volume is entitled *Augustus*, but is, in effect, a
picture of Augustus and his times. The elaborate
study of the Emperor's career and psychology is part
of a wider panorama in which the whole life of the
civilized world during the most wonderful century of
human history is painted in brilliant colours. Lord
Tweedsmuir excels in characterization, and his careful
character sketches and literary appreciations add much
to the interest of his book. At the end the reader is

conducted round the Roman Empire as it existed under the Augustan peace, an Empire without racialism or religious persecution, or tariff barriers, or communism or fascism; when Spain enjoyed the happiest period of her history; when Syria supported a population of ten millions; when North Africa and Egypt were active seminaries of intellectual life; when twelve hundred armed men at Lyons sufficed to police all Gaul; an Empire in which liberty was combined with order. In a notable concluding passage Lord Tweedsmuir speculates upon the reflections which might be aroused in the mind of Augustus were his *magna imago* to return to earth.

'He would be puzzled at some of our experiments in empire, and might well complain that the imperfections of his work were taken as its virtues, and that so many truths had gone silently out of mind. He had prided himself on having given the world peace, and he would be amazed by the loud praise of war as a natural and wholesome concomitant of a nation's life. Wars he had fought from an anxious desire to safeguard his people, as the shepherd builds the defences of his sheepfold; but he hated the thing, because he knew well the deadly "disordering" which the Greek historian noted as the consequence of the most triumphant campaign. He would marvel, too, at the current talk of racial purity, the exaltation of one breed of men as the chosen favourites of the gods. . . . But chiefly, I think, he would be perplexed by the modern passion for regimentation and the assumed contradiction between law and liberty. . . . And when this expert in mechanism observed the craving of great peoples to enslave themselves and to exult hysterically in their bonds, bewilderment would harden to disdain in his masterful eyes.'

III

THE WHIG HISTORIANS[1]

UNTIL recent years the character of our medieval constitution was ill-understood. Even the most important objects of traditional veneration, such as Magna Carta and the Jury and the medieval Parliament, were conceived under a misleading light. Few people realized how little of democracy there was in the Charter, how much of monarchy in the régime of the Jury, or how little of legislation in the work of our early Parliaments. Even Bishop Stubbs, whose mind was free of the political prepossessions of the seventeenth century, did not fully appreciate what the great Charter meant or how a parliament in the first years of the fourteenth century transacted its business. The key to the clearer understanding of these mysteries was not supplied until the study of constitutional history was reinforced by that closer interpretation of English legal documents of which Maitland was in this country the master and the pioneer.

The scientific study of our constitutional antiquities was prejudiced by the immense regard which Englishmen of every political complexion were disposed to attach to tradition. When precedents began to count in practical politics, they cease to count in the forum of science. In the political struggles of the seventeenth

[1] Reprinted from *Proceedings of the British Academy*, vol. xiv, 1928.

century each party appealed to precedent, each party believed that its action was conformable to the law and constitution of the kingdom and levelled at its antagonist the hated charge of innovation. 'During a whole long course of years', observes Macaulay, 'every Whig historian was anxious to prove that the old English government was all but republican, every Tory historian to prove that it was all but despotic.' The truth was that it was neither the one thing nor the other, but a shifting balance of forces and a storehouse of conflicting precedents.

In the course of the eighteenth century a change came over the intellectual atmosphere of Whig society. The old polemics based on black-letter learning, which had delighted Prynne and other antiquarians during the Civil War, ceased to have a meaning after the supremacy of Parliament had been established by 'the glorious Revolution'. The Whig party broke its connexion with Puritanism. It became less narrow, more worldly wise and more tolerant. The virtues and vices incidental to adversity disappeared and were replaced by the pleasant self-assurance and optimism which come so naturally to easy-going Englishmen with a long spell of assured influence and power. Newton and Locke stood for the new spirit in philosophy, the Bank of England for the enlarged scale of private and public wealth. The Constitution was idolized by writers like De Lolme and Blackstone, who, though they failed to perceive the emergence of Cabinet government, trod for the most part on the solid ground of ascertained constitutional practice.

Everything seemed to be going well. The Jacobite danger was exorcized, an empire was won in India and Canada, and the wealth of the country was steadily mounting. A constitution under which these happy things were possible seemed to be a pearl of great price.

From these dogmatic slumbers England was aroused by a religious revival, an unsuccessful war, a challenge to the accepted philosophy of trade and a great philanthropic agitation. When Wesley and Whitfield had done their best and the Americans their worst, when the doctrines of the *Wealth of Nations* had begun to affect the minds of public men in London and the slave-traders of Bristol and Liverpool had been driven from their entrenchments, England was a changed world. A stock of new and exciting ideas had been accumulated in the country. A constitution under which an empire could be lost, a king could purchase or bully a parliament, a city like Manchester could be unrepresented in the House of Commons, and Mr. Rigby could make a fortune out of the floating balances of the army, could no longer be regarded as sacrosanct by intelligent men. Grave and eloquent voices had begun to call everything in question, the Parliamentary suffrage, economic reform, the trade policy, religious disabilities, how India should be governed or Ireland appeased, when the long and desperate war against Revolutionary and Imperial France imposed a moratorium on political progress.

There was one question of far-ranging importance which, seeing that it transcended the ordinary divisions of party politics, was not allowed to go into winter quarters during the Napoleonic war. The agitation for the abolition, first of the Slave Trade and then, when this object had been achieved, of slavery itself, was pursued with unabated energy both in Parliament and in the country by Wilberforce and his devoted band of followers. These ardent men were not of the common tribe of politicians. They cared nothing for the prizes of public life or for the game of parliamentary controversy. Drawing their inspiration from the deepest of all fountains they pursued with a single eye their grand object of striking the fetters from the slave and spreading Christianity among the pagans. By their contemporaries they were known as the Saints. Though many of them were evangelical members of the Church of England, who ordinarily voted with the Tories, by their zeal for public education, by their freedom from sectarian prejudice, and by the skill with which they organized and kept on foot a great democratic agitation, they did more to accustom the mind of the country to the idea of change than all the official leaders of the Whig party.

It was in this atmosphere of ardent concern for great causes that Macaulay passed his childhood. His father, Zachary Macaulay, was one of the Clapham saints, and, like his master Wilberforce, dedicated to the great task of uprooting slavery and spreading the knowledge of the Bible through the world. It would be difficult to conceive a home better calculated to form the spirit of a great national historian. Clapham, which is now distinguished only as a railway junction, was then the power-house of a great humanitarian movement. The young Macaulay grew up to the sound of earnest men debating large issues of public policy. Members of Parliament flitted backwards and forwards bringing intelligence of bills, resolutions, and manœuvres. The house was open to the professors of every kind of Protestant belief. The boy was thus early initiated into the variety of English life, its diverse groupings and affinities, its cross currents of interests, its secluded backwaters of religious zeal and eccentricity, and the way in which great masses of sinister opinion could be assailed and defeated. Though his passion for literature carried him far away from the range of his parents' habitual thoughts and interests, he could not, with such a home, be insensible to the great public questions of the hour or of the part which a man should endeavour to play. He was taught to be disinterested and to expect the same high standard of others.

His precocity was amazing but not, perhaps, an unmixed advantage, for as he filled his childish imagination with the figures of the past, he conceived them with such ardour and distinctness that it was difficult for him ever to reshape these first impressions. What he felt about Oliver Cromwell at ten, he felt about him at fifty. His imaginary world was made so fast and at so high a temperature of conviction that it surrounded him through life. Not so does the modern youth, imbued with the delicacies of the psychological novel, approach the task of describing historical characters.

As he grew to manhood he witnessed the renewal of those political activities and aspirations which had been long suspended under the régime of Tory repression, the reform of the penal laws, the removal of religious disabilities, the revision of trade policy, the agitation for parliamentary reform. It was inevitable that a youth of his generous vehemence should throw in his lot with the party of movement. At Cambridge he becomes a Whig, and finds a hero in William III. At twenty-five he contributes to the *Edinburgh Review*, the great Whig organ, that article on Milton which made him famous.

Four years later he brought up a number of Cambridge Whigs from London to vote for Catholic emancipation and turned the election. At the age of thirty he entered Parliament as the Whig member for the little borough of Calne, which was placed at his disposal by the Marquis of Lansdowne. From the first he caught the ear of the House of Commons. His brilliance took London by storm, and Holland House, with its imperious mistress no less than its charming master, the nephew of Charles James Fox and the pious guardian of his memory, was at his feet.

A youth of generous aspirations who prepares himself to take a part in the public life of his country is never at a loss for a hero. Macaulay's hero was Sir James Mackintosh, a Scot thirty-five years his senior, who left upon his contemporaries a rare impression of goodness, knowledge, and power. Mackintosh was a Whig who began life as a firebrand and ended as a sage. In 1830, when Macaulay entered Parliament, Mackintosh was a man of sixty-five with a full career of honourable public activity behind him. At the age of twenty-six he had crossed swords with Burke over the French Revolution. At twenty-seven he became secretary of the Friends of the People, the earliest English Association for the promotion of Parliamentary Reform. Ten years later as counsel for Peltier he had given eloquent expression to the view that England was and should be allowed to remain the asylum of free thought and free expression in a Europe generally enslaved by the authority of Napoleon. After a period of Indian service as Recorder of Bombay, Mackintosh returned to London and entered the House of Commons. His orations against the repressive laws, in support of the recognition of the South American Republics and in favour of religious toleration, his expression of sympathy for the victims of Austrian tyranny in Italy, his powerful and entirely sound refutation of the argument that the King's coronation oath was a bar to legislation in relief of the Catholics, won for him a success of esteem from his political associates. The cause, however, with which he was more particularly identified during the twenties was the reform of our penal law. In this humane and much needed branch of social reform Mackintosh was the associate and successor of Romilly.

There are generally one or two men in public life whose influence is not to be measured by their parlia-

mentary attainments. Mackintosh was one of these.
As a House of Commons man he held a position of
secondary prominence, 'a respectable ally', as Hazlitt
observes, 'but not a very formidable opponent', a
lecturer rather than an orator and with too much
of the savant in his composition and too little im-
petuosity of feeling to achieve the highest parliamentary success. The House of Commons, however,
always recognizes character. Mackintosh was sincere,
copious in distinguished vocabulary, and endowed
with the Scottish capacity for stating a principle. If,
for instance, he had occasion to talk about the civil
government of Canada, he would not lose himself in a
maze of Canadian detail. He would say, 'My maxims
of colonial policy are few and simple—a full and sufficient protection from all foreign influence, full permission to conduct the whole of their internal affairs
. . . no restrictions of any kind upon the industry and
traffic of the people.' And as he had great learning
and a memory described by Macaulay, who had a
right to pronounce upon memories, as 'the most
capacious and accurately constructed that any human
being possessed', and was ready, albeit a man of real
humility of character, to express complete and considered views on every topic which might emerge,
he was a most instructive and agreeable companion
wherever the gifts of the spirit are valued. People had
resort to him as to an oracle. He had been trained for
a doctor, had been a lawyer in London and a judge in
Bombay, was a good deal of an historian, something
of a philosopher and at least half a statesman, and

his conversation, which was animated and without pedantry, was enriched by all these tributaries. When Macaulay first made his acquaintance Mackintosh was embarked upon a history of England from 1688 to 1789, and was gathering that noble assemblage of extracts from the public and private collections of the period which was subsequently placed at the disposal of the younger historian. 'The judgement', writes Macaulay, 'with which Sir James in great masses of the richest ore of history selected what was valuable and rejected what was worthless can be fully appreciated only by one who toiled after him in the same vein.'[1]

The scale and quality of these preparations are of themselves evidence of Mackintosh's historical abilities, but of his projected work there remains only a popular history contributed to Lardner's *Encyclopaedia* and that admirable fragment (posthumously published) on the reign of James II, which furnished the occasion for Macaulay's essay. In the view of Jeffrey, an ardent admirer, the historical remains of Mackintosh were sufficient to class him with Voltaire and Montesquieu. Macaulay is more moderate in his encomium. While commending his friend for the just respect with which he wrote of the Whigs of the Revolution, he finds that there is perhaps too much disquisition and too little narrative in the work. There was, indeed, too much disquisition altogether in Mackintosh, and too little of order, industry, and concentration.

[1] *History of England*, c. iii.

Among the distinguished men who frequented the gatherings at Holland House while Macaulay was rising to eminence, there was a scholar, less conspicuous in general conversational power than Mackintosh and a good deal less important to Macaulay, but in his own wide sphere of historical and literary knowledge the first authority in the country. This was Henry Hallam, whose *Constitutional History of England*, first published in 1827, was welcomed by Macaulay as the most impartial book that he had ever read. No praise can be too high for the learning, the accuracy, and the integrity of Hallam, but he was a Whig, and his book, though entirely free from party passion, is informed from start to finish by Whig principles. It is perhaps only a Whig who, in comparing the claims of the two parties, would declare that the Whigs had 'a natural tendency to political improvement, the Tories an aversion from it', and again that the Whigs appear to have taken a 'far more comprehensive view of the nature and ends of civil society than their opponents', that 'their principles were more virtuous, more flexible to the variations of time and circumstance, more congenial to large and masculine intellects'; but then after bestowing this high commendation upon the tenets of the party to which he belongs Hallam proceeds very properly to observe that 'it is one thing to prefer the Whig principle, another to justify or to advocate the party which bore that name'. Hallam is successful in observing this valuable distinction. He can find fault with Whiggish men and Whiggish measures. In the greatest of all

the transactions with which he has to deal, the outbreak of the Great Rebellion, he passes censure upon
the Long Parliament for putting its cause to the
doubtful arbitrament of war. He refuses to accept the
famous outburst attributed to Chatham. 'There was
ambition, there was sedition, there was violence; but
no man shall persuade us that it was not the cause of
liberty on one side and of tyranny on the other.' In
his cool, fair-minded way he points out that on the
one side there was 'little of such liberty as a wise man
would hold dear', and that on the other he was 'not
yet convinced that the peers and gentry of England
were combating on the side of tyranny'. Macaulay,
as we know, found him too cool and judicial, too
indulgent to Queen Elizabeth and to Charles I, too
critical of the Long Parliament. Certainly it was not
in Hallam's manner to describe the English Reformation as 'a work which had been begun by Henry, the
murderer of his wives, was continued by Somerset,
the murderer of his brother, and completed by Elizabeth, the murderer of her guest'. He preferred to
strike when the iron was cold.

It has been well said by a modern writer that Hallam
imagined that there was an English constitution and
that the first two Stuarts broke it.[1] The air of certainty
with which Hallam invests the principles of the constitution in the seventeenth century is one of those
retrospective illusions to which historians are prone.
The precedents did not all point one way. The ex-

[1] G. P. Gooch, *History and Historians in the Nineteenth
Century*, 1923.

pedient which ultimately proved to be the true solution of the constitutional problem was divined by neither party. No one foresaw the Cabinet, which grew up in the dark. On either side suspicions and fears were overdrawn, for no King can be a true despot without a standing army, and the concessions demanded by Puritan and Parliamentary feeling could have been made without injury to the dynasty or the Crown. It may be urged against Hallam that he makes insufficient allowance for the obscurities and uncertainties of a time in which new problems were placing an uncomfortable strain on the old fabric, and does not attempt to share the emotions of our ancestors. His attitude is that of a magistrate judging a case. 'Every popular assembly', he observes, 'truly zealous for a great cause will display more heat and passion than cool-blooded men after the lapse of centuries may approve.' Hallam is the cool-blooded man and his approval is carefully husbanded.

In one respect Hallam differs fron the Whig historians whose work is here reviewed. Macaulay said of Fox and Mackintosh that they shared one eminent qualification for writing history. They had 'spoken history, acted history, lived history'. It was not so with Hallam. Though he had been called to the bar and mixed in high Whig society, Hallam never took an active part in politics. His is the case, happily not infrequent in our country, of the man of private fortune and ample leisure who devotes his life to literary pursuits. It may be that what such a man loses in momentum he gains in accuracy; but if so, accuracy is

bought high. Hallam's political principles were domi-
nated by caution, and as in his *Constitutional History*
he is at pains to warn his readers that the English
Revolution of 1688 was the result of a chapter of
singular accidents unlikely to recur, so when he was
faced with the Reform Bill he shrank from it with
aversion. So mild and temperate was his Whiggism
that in the extension of the franchise to the middle-
class he descried the seeds of revolution.

If Macaulay was fortunate in the influences of his
childhood and youth, he was also happily inspired in
the order and sequence of his activities. Some men
attack their *magnum opus* too soon, others postpone it
too late. Macaulay was thirty-eight years of age when
he embarked upon his *History of England*. He was
then at the summit of his splendid powers and energies
and a rich experience of life and letters lay behind
him. He had won the ear of the House of Commons
as an orator and had settled for the vast population
of British India the form of their penal law and the
shape of their public education. His reading in the
memorials of classical antiquity and in the literature
of France, Italy, and England during the seventeenth
and eighteenth centuries would have done credit to
an industrious professor and was amazing in a public
man. His pen also was thoroughly exercised in those
flashing contributions to periodical literature which,
though far inferior to the *History* and only intended for an ephemeral effect, were so remarkable
as to bring enduring fame to their author and to

secure for him grateful readers in every part of the
globe.

Clio is a jealous and a grudging mistress. For
a period of eight years Macaulay's allegiance was
divided between the composition of the *History* and
the exacting duties of a prominent member of Parliament, who whenever he rose to speak filled the House
to overcrowding, and when his own party were in
power was called upon to share in the task of government. The result was unfortunate for the *History*.
When death came suddenly to him at the age of fifty-
nine, the period most congenial to his taste and with
respect to which his preliminary information was most
complete had not been reached. In compensation
there are the classic orations on the Sugar Duties and
the Law of Copyright, but how gladly would posterity
exchange a dozen brilliant Parliamentary speeches for
Macaulay's history of the reign of Queen Anne.

In an early essay (May 1828) he had laid out his
conception of the manner in which the perfect history
should be written. 'Our historians', he observes,
'practise the art of controversy but neglect the art of
narrative.' Hume was an accomplished advocate.
Gibbon deserved 'some censure'. Mitford 'substan-
tially violates truth on every page'. Out of regard to
a false convention of dignity 'the noiseless and name-
less revolutions of the past' were not recorded.[1] A
truly great historian would reclaim those materials
which the novelist has appropriated, and endeavour
to represent the spirit of an age in miniature. 'He

[1] *Misc. Works*, i. 272 ff.

must see ordinary men as they appear in their ordinary desires and their ordinary pleasures. He must mingle in the crowds of the exchange and the coffee-house. . . . He must not shrink from exploring even the retreats of misery.' Macaulay then resolved to restore to history the charm and humour of narrative which had been lost in a reflective and critical age. The story would provide its own lessons. Only from an intimate knowledge of the domestic life of nations, such as a full narrative could supply, could the statesman attain to a prognosis of political events.

In the year in which he put pen to paper upon the history of England Macaulay thus defined his political faith to the electors of Edinburgh (May 28, 1839):

'I entered public life a Whig and a Whig I still remain. When I use the word I use it in no narrowed sense. I mean by a Whig, not a man who subscribes implicitly to all the contents of any book, though the writer were Locke, or to the dicta of any statesman, though that statesman were Fox, or to any party, although composed of the finest and noblest spirits of the ages. It seems to me I can discern a great party often depressed but never extinguished, preserving its constant identity, a party which, though often tainted with the sins of the age, was always in advance of it, a party which, though guilty of some crimes and errors, has done its best to promote civil freedom, religious toleration, civilization and social improvement; and of that party I am proud to acknowledge myself a member. That was the party, gentlemen, which in the great question of monopolies stood up against Elizabeth; that was the party which in the reign of James I organized for the first time a Parliamentary opposition, and gradually advanced the privileges of the people; that party drove Charles I from the menaces of the ship-money,

destroyed the iniquitous Star Chamber; under Charles II
gave us the Habeas Corpus Act, and brought about the
Revolution of 1688; that was the party which broke the yoke
of the tyrannical Church in this country and saved Scotland
from the deplorable fate of Ireland; that party maintained
the constitutional throne of the House of Hanover, against
the hostility of the rich Catholic nobility and gentry of
England, and the designs of the Pretender; that was the party
which opposed the American war in the eighteenth century,
and through whose exertions in the nineteenth civil liberty
was obtained to the Catholic and freedom to trade in corn
was advocated and the slave trade abolished. Whatever, then,
has been done for the amelioration of the condition of the
people, for the modification of the penal laws, has been all
done by that party, and of that party I repeat, I am a
member.'

It was a high claim eloquently stated. To recount
the historical claims of a party, to whose exertions his
country owed so much, was a task worthy of his enthusiasm. His original design was in his own words
to give 'an entire view of all the transactions which
took place between the Revolution which brought
the Crown into harmony with the Parliament and the
Revolution which brought the Parliament into harmony with the nation'. 'I really do not think', he
writes on November 5, 1841, 'that there is in our
literature so great a void as that which I am trying to
supply. English History from 1688 to the French
Revolution is even to educated people almost a *terra
incognita*. I will venture to say that it is quite an even
chance whether even such a man as Simpson, or Senior,
can repeat accurately the names of the Prime-ministers

of that period. The materials for an amusing narrative are immense. I shall not be satisfied unless I produce something which shall for a few days supersede the last fashionable novel on the tables of young ladies.'

The first two volumes appeared in December 1848 and conclude with an apostrophe to the English Revolution which is contrasted to its advantage with the revolutions which had recently broken out in the continent of Europe. 'Now if ever', he writes, 'we ought to be able to appreciate the whole importance of the stand which was made by our forefathers against the House of Stuart. All round us the world is convulsed with the agonies of great nations. It is because we had a preserving revolution in the seventeenth century that we have not had a destroying revolution in the nineteenth. It is because we had freedom in the midst of servitude that we have order in the midst of anarchy.'

The subject grew in his hands. If two volumes had been required to bring the story down to the deposition of James, how could the reign of William the liberator be compressed into a shorter space? The idea of carrying the history down to the death of George IV was given up.

'I have now', he writes in his Journal (Feb. 8, 1849) 'made up my mind to change my plan about my history. I will first set myself to know the whole subject; to get, by reading and travelling, a full acquaintance with William's reign. I reckon that it will take me eighteen months to do this. I must visit Holland, Belgium, Scotland, Ireland, France. The Dutch archives and French archives must be ransacked.

I will see whether anything is to be got from other diplomatic collections. I must see Londonderry, the Boyne, Aughrim, Limerick, Kinsale, Namur again, Landen, Steinkirk. I must turn over hundreds, thousands of pamphlets. Lambeth, the Bodleian and the other Oxford Libraries, the Devonshire Papers, the British Museum must be explored and notes made: and then I shall go to work.'

A vast programme. When he died in 1859 he had not reached the end of William's reign.

It may be doubted whether any book in any language treating of a period of modern history has brought so much fresh and important information into the view of the general reader or has so victoriously stood the test of time. On the last point Sir Charles Firth, who of all living scholars best knows the evidence upon which Macaulay worked, speaks with incontestable authority. In his preface to the illustrated edition of the history of England Sir Charles writes thus: 'The task of illustrating the history necessitated a close scrutiny of Macaulay's pages and while it made some defects and omissions more apparent, it has increased rather than diminished my admiration for what Macaulay succeeded in doing.'

One thing which he has succeeded in doing is by a great effort of learning and imagination and literary craftsmanship to revive for us the lives of our forefathers in the later half of the seventeenth century; and in doing this to set an entirely new standard of diligent curiosity for the imitation of subsequent historians. It is not merely the bulk of the authorities consulted which impresses the reader of Macaulay's

History, but their astonishing range and variety.
Plays, sermons, ballads, fly-sheets, pamphlets, however ephemeral, take their place with the statutes,
memoirs, state papers, and private correspondence
which form the staple diet of the historical student.
For his famous description of England at the accession
of James II he consults the drawings of English landscape made for the Grand Duke Cosimo, as well as
books on birds, plants, animals, and roads and every
description of topographical and statistical record
upon which he can lay his hands. Smith's *Ancient and
Modern State of the County of Kerry*, published in
1786, 'than which I have never met with a better book
of the kind and size', supplied him with the particulars
which were worked up in the delightful picture of
that beautiful county (rendered specially interesting
to him from its associations with the Lansdowne
family), which is one of the little gems in the twelfth
chapter. He walked four times round the walls of
Londonderry before writing his enthralling account
of the siege. 'An absurd tragi-comedy acted in some
low theatre in 1689 or 1690' is adduced as illustration
of the view of Ireland which was taken by Englishmen
in the reign of James II. 'A rare lampoon' sheds a ray
of contemporary light on the coronation of William
and Mary. Extracts are procured from the municipal records of Inverness. The Union and College
Libraries at Oxford and Cambridge, the Advocates'
Library in Edinburgh, the Royal Irish Academy, the
great country houses like Woburn, Welbeck, and
Bowood, the national repositories in Paris, at the

Hague, and in London are made to yield up their treasures. 'There is', he writes, 'a noble and I suppose unique collection of newspapers of William's reign in the British Museum. I have turned over every page of that collection.' It was in fact no distinction to be read by Macaulay, for he devoured most things, and what he devoured he retained.

Another great excellence of his history is that, although it deals in great detail with a comparatively short period, it furnishes the best general introduction to the understanding of English history and English political life which has ever been written. Macaulay was no specialist. He knew English history from end to end, some periods a great deal better than others but all periods better than the average well-educated man. His opening survey of the course of English history up to the Restoration could hardly be improved upon as an outline of governing tendencies and factors; and when, as he proceeds on his course, we exchange broad generalizations for a minute narrative, we are never left without direction. We know whence we have come and we are made to feel whither the forces of the time are taking us. Unlike S. R. Gardiner, who worked up his history upon a strictly chronological plan in order to avoid the error of imputing to his actors knowledge which they could not or might not possess, Macaulay revels in exhibiting the significance of the transactions which he recounts, as his wide knowledge of the later history of England enables him to do in an instructive and illuminating way.

It may be interesting to dwell for a moment upon a few cases in which a happy use is made of knowledge either belonging to a subsequent age or contained in sources of a later date than that with which the author is for the time being concerned. After explaining the fortunate circumstance that a standing army was for a long time connected in the imagination of Royalists and Prelatists with regicide and field preaching, he goes on to say that as late as the year 1786 a minister who enjoyed no common measure of the confidence of the Tories found it impossible to overcome their aversion to his scheme for fortifying the coast. It would be difficult to impress more clearly upon the reader the extreme unpopularity of standing armies in the reign of Charles II than by this proof of the survival of the same feeling a hundred years later among the members of that party in the State who, on general grounds, might be expected to be most immune from it. A touch hardly less happy occurs in a foot-note to a paragraph on the condition of the Anglican clergy under Charles II. It will be remembered that Macaulay, relying partly on Eachard's *Causes of the Contempt of the Clergy* and partly on a vast mass of light contemporary literature, depicts the country clergy of that period in a most unfavourable light and the whole profession as suffering a social eclipse. Macaulay's portrait has been criticized with some justice as being unduly sombre; but some support is given to his contention by a letter of Warburton to Hurd of July 5, 1752, which contains the significant sentence, 'Our grandees have at last found their way back into the Church'. Fashion and virtue are not synonymous; but, if the Church was just beginning to be fashionable again in the middle of the eighteenth century, it is reasonable to suppose that its social consideration was impaired in the preceding period.

If Macaulay was a strong party man, he was free from the worst defects of the partisan spirit. His manly good nature and strong Scottish common sense saved him from the infirmities of the political sectary. He was too great a patriot, too much alive to the splendours of our national inheritance, to put the interests of a party before the welfare of the nation. He happened, however, to believe with all the strength of his nature that the Whig revolution of 1688 had been the main source of the happy progress of his country and of its widespread influence throughout the world. He believed that it had saved us from the spiritual dominion of Rome and a subservient relation to the powerful monarchy of France, that it had placed the reign of law above tyrannical caprice, that it had secured the freedom and independence of parliamentary government, that it had initiated the régime of religious toleration, and put an end to a terrible period of civil strife and proscription. Holding these views and believing that William of Orange and the Whig party were the chief instruments by which Britain was rid of great dangers and placed upon the road to enlightenment and affluence, he deployed all his energies and powers in giving illustration to the faith which was in him. Even if his natural candour and honesty had not forbidden him to garble evidence, he would have thought his case too convincing to need questionable supports. He could afford to give points to the enemy with a liberal hand, to exhibit the political profligacy of the Whig exclusionists, to pillory the inventions of Oates, to relate, though not without pain, how his hero William divided between two foreigners an extent of country larger than Hertfordshire, and to point out that upon the question of the Catholic Celts of Ireland the Tory Dr. Johnson was far more liberal than his intolerant Whig contemporaries. The strong lights and shades of the book are not mainly due to Macaulay's politics but to his perfervid Scottish nature, to that 'vehemence and self-confidence' which his father had reproved in him when he was a boy of fourteen and had vainly hoped might one day be replaced in him by 'the ornament of a meek and quiet spirit'. He was a man quick to take hearty likes and dislikes, the vigour of which was entirely unaffected by his distance in time from the object. High Churchmen deplore his handling of Laud, but even had he known all that the Dean of Winchester knows about that prelate, he would still have disliked him, not for his opinions chiefly, but for what he was. There were certain qualities in a man, or a book, or a work of art from which he turned with instinctive aversion, as from an evil smell. Anything morbid, anything mystical, anything dark or confused or tormented, anything grotesque or dreamy or out of perspective, he rejected at once. Whether natures which contained these elements were Whig or Tory did not matter; they were not pleasing to

Macaulay. He condemned the morbid self-examination of Laud for the same reason that he is repelled by the wild enthusiasm of George Fox, by the Chinese porcelain at Hampton Court, and by the whole range of Indian sacred literature. It was not Whiggism which made him thus, but the overflowing happiness of 'a wholesome, ardent, hard-headed, limited Scot.

He was so happy and inwardly composed that he could not enter into the spirit of Puritanism, one of the principal fountain-heads from which the stream of Whig political thinking has descended. In this respect Carlyle, who did not much like happy men, and was once uncivil enough to describe Macaulay as 'a poor Holland House unbeliever with spectacles instead of eyes',[1] was more successful than the great Whig historian. A tender compassion for inward spiritual torments was not among Macaulay's spiritual graces; but he was right to dislike the gloom and harsh intolerance of the Puritans. For all forms of religious extravagance his distaste was such that he, the son of Zachary Macaulay, actually permitted himself to speak of the 'bray of Exeter Hall'.

Wherever he found a touch of the manly or heroic his sympathies went out towards it. He had no liking for Romanism, though he possessed a sound general knowledge of its historical credentials, and, of all manifestations of Romanism, the Jesuit Order was least to his taste. Yet he cannot conclude his exposition of the reasons which led to a widespread distrust of Jesuit morality in the later half of the seventeenth

[1] J. A. Froude, *Thomas Carlyle*, vol. i, p. 192.

century without going out of his way to pay a splendid tribute to the spirit of heroic self-sacrifice which that order of devoted men had displayed from time to time throughout their history. The passage is well known but will bear repetition.

'When in our own time a new and terrible pestilence passed round the globe, when in some great cities fear had dissolved all the ties which hold society together, when the secular clergy had deserted their flocks, when medical succour was not to be purchased by gold, when the strongest natural affections had yielded to the love of life, even then the Jesuit was found by the pallet which bishop and curate, physician and nurse, father and mother had deserted, bending over infected lips to catch the faint accents of confession, and holding up to the last, before the expiring penitent, the image of the expiring Redeemer.'[1]

It will also be conceded to Macaulay that he does not for a moment endeavour to ascribe to the progenitors of the Whig movement in England virtues which they cannot claim. His thesis is that the standard of virtue and honour among our public men was at its lowest point in William's reign. The Revolution 'of all revolutions the least violent, of all revolutions the most beneficent' was not the work of high-minded and disinterested statesmen. The moral which Macaulay draws for his readers is not that the age which witnessed 'the glorious Revolution' was better than his own, but that it was far worse, that by every standard by which the happiness and virtue of a society can be measured the England of the Reform

[1] *History of England*, c. vi.

Act was to be preferred to the England of the Bill of Rights, and that the more carefully the history of any past age is examined the more reason we have to congratulate ourselves that we live in the present.

An apparent exception to the rule of progress is afforded by the history of Parliamentary corruption. The votes of members of the House of Commons were bought and sold more freely under the Whig administration of the blameless Pelham than under the Tory Clifford, who initiated this bad system in the days of the Cabal. On this Macaulay observes that, if the English in the time of George II had really been more sordid and dishonest than their forefathers, the deterioration would not have shown itself in one place alone. The progress of judicial venality and official venality would have kept pace with the progress of Parliamentary venality. But nothing, he concludes, is more certain than that while the legislature was becoming more and more venal, the Courts of Law and the public offices were becoming purer and purer. This is a good instance of Macaulay's ability to take a large and balanced view of the facts of human progress.

In a letter to his friend Napier quoted in Sir George Trevelyan's famous biography of his uncle, Macaulay says that he had never written a page of criticism on poetry or the fine arts which he would not burn if he had the power, and that though he had a strong and acute enjoyment of works of the imagination he had never habituated himself to dissect them. When he liked a play or a poem he conceived a kind of animal

rapture for it and he would not diminish his enjoyment by attempting to assess the precise measure of
his delight. But if aesthetic criticism was not within
his compass, political criticism was. He had a great
gift for picking out what was historically important in
the transactions of the past and what was politically
wise. He was the first writer fully to apprehend the
significance of the history of the Licensing Act, and
to note that 'from the day on which the emancipation
of our literature was accomplished, the purification
of our literature began'. No previous author had
devoted adequate attention to the early stages of
Cabinet government in the reign of William III, or
assigned to the Sunderland ministry its true significance in the history of English constitutional development. Considering the very strong opinions which he
entertained with respect to the political problems of
his own time, he was remarkably successful in his
resistance to the temptation to apply the remedies of
the nineteenth century to the ailments of the seventeenth. The ardent advocate of Lord Grey's Reform
Bill remarks that, if Parliamentary Reform had been
introduced in 1692, it would have favoured the Tories,
led to a restoration of the Stuarts, a persecution of
the dissenters, and would probably have obstructed
Union with Scotland. A champion of religious toleration might have been expected to lament the failure
of the Comprehension Bill of 1689, the original parch-
ment of which Macaulay discovered in the archives
of the House of Lords. Macaulay, however, shrewdly
notes that the Independents, the Baptists, and the

Quakers, who probably then formed the majority of the Nonconformist body, would in the circumstances have been excluded, and that if the High Church party had not defeated the Bill in Convocation, the country would probably have lost its civil and religious liberty.

There is, however, a better illustration still of Macaulay's power of disengaging the past from the present. He observes that people whose minds were under the influence of the struggle for Catholic emancipation found a difficulty in seeing the events of 1687 and 1688 in a perfectly correct light. Eldon, whose view was that religious disabilities were always useful and necessary, represented one fallacy. The other, 'which was not altogether without influence even on an intellect so calm and philosophical as that of Mackintosh', was that religious disabilities could never have been useful or necessary. Macaulay's doctrine, of course, was that these disabilities were useful under James II and harmful under George III. The amount of toleration which was accorded under the Toleration Act was neither too much nor too little, but exactly adapted to the needs of the moment. Nothing can illustrate more completely the angle from which the historically-minded Whigs viewed affairs than the following observations upon the English manner in legislation which are evoked by that curiously illogical but most effective and beneficent statute.

'To think nothing of symmetry and much of convenience; never to remove an anomaly merely because it is an anomaly; never to innovate except where some grievance is felt; never to innovate except so far as to get rid of the grievance; never to lay down any proposition of wider extent than the particular case for which it is necessary to provide; these are the rules which have from the days of John to the days of Queen Victoria generally guided the deliberations of our two hundred and fifty Parliaments.'

Psychology, if not the whole, is an important part of politics. The statesman must know what men want and how they think and by what means they may be persuaded to accept his direction. Of this rough kind of psychological knowledge Macaulay has an ample sufficiency. His interpretations of individual character may lack delicacy and depth, though they are not, save in rare instances, without practical insight or unsustained by evidence; and he has a gift for psychological generalization. The long popularity of the royal cure for scrofula is well explained in the phrase 'Nothing is so credulous as misery'. The curious but quite intelligible fact that people who make a great sacrifice for principle should be unable to persevere in the daily practice of obscure virtues is illustrated from the lives of the Nonjurors and the Epistle of St. Cyprian. In his sense of the psychology of crowds and of the part which highly simplified forms of hate and prejudice play in popular movements at critical times he challenges the author of *Barnaby Rudge*. His errors on the subject of William Penn are notorious. He may have been wrong in his diagnosis of Marlborough, and too harsh to James II and Dryden; but in the interpretation of the wider movements of history he does not go far astray. He can put Scottish

Jacobitism in its place, exhibit the old Gaelic institutions of Scotland with a great deal more regard to the truth than had been shown by the detractors or the romantic enthusiasts, and enable his readers to understand how by its alliance with the native Irishry, 'of all foreigners the most detested and despised', the House of Stuart came to irretrievable ruin.

A distinguished member of this Academy has written with an authority which I cannot command of the limitations of Macaulay's knowledge;[1] and the student who consults the *Bibliography of British History for the Stuart Period*, recently edited by Professor Godfrey Davies for the Clarendon Press, will be able to measure the new sources of information which the progress of historical industry has placed at our disposal. There are books which Macaulay might have read, documents which he left for subsequent investigators to unearth. In his treatment of foreign policy and of fiscal history he has left gaps of which, being somewhat disposed to the view that what he did not know was not knowledge, he appears to have been wholly unconscious.[2] Yet it is absurd to censure him for his failure to know everything, as, for instance, those reports by F. Bonnet from the Berlin archives, of which von Ranke makes so large a use in the only full narrative of the period by a first-rate historical scholar which has so far been given to the world. There is a fallacy in the assumption that the more a

[1] G. P. Gooch, *History and Historians of the Nineteenth Century*.

[2] C. H. Firth, *A Commentary on Macaulay's History of England*, 1938.

man reads the more nearly he approaches to the truth. There is no such relation between the thing that was and the number of words which have been written about it. It is even more probable that a good history will emerge from a few first-class authorities cleverly interpreted by a fresh mind than from a vast and exhausting miscellany of unequal value. Macaulay did not explore the German archives. Only a few letters from the correspondence of William III with Heinsius were before him; but in the reports of the Dutch envoys in London he possessed an excellent source of information; and from these and many other witnesses he extracted with amazing skill a convincing image of the march of events. Beside his lifelike pictures of the men and women of that age, the figures who move across the pages of the Prussian savant are dim and bloodless phantoms.

The reputation of Macaulay as an historian has suffered not a little from the survival and republication of his essays, more particularly of such essays as were written in youth before he went out to India. He should be judged not by the Edinburgh essays, in which he avowedly forced the note in order to make an impression during the short life of a periodical magazine, but by his *History*. All the essays are brilliant, but in some accuracy is sacrificed to effect, while others are marred by blunders or the bias of temperament or party feeling. In the *History*, composed for distant posterity, the blemishes are fewer and less apparent, while the merits discernible in the essays shine with an equal or a greater lustre. There

is no part of the History which has suffered so much
from the criticism of later historians as has the essay
on Warren Hastings. Yet the merits even of this, the
most sharply censured of his shorter pieces, are so
conspicuous, that no student of the history of British
rule in India omits to read what Macaulay has there
written or, having read it, fails to gain a juster appreciation of Hastings himself, of the wide sweep and
extraordinary character of his responsibilities and
powers, and of the confidence and attachment which
he inspired in vast masses of human beings.

A robust English patriotism was a common attribute of the Whig school of historians. They shared
the elation of the great triumph over Napoleon and
believed that in the Parliamentary system as developed
and practised by Whigs a sovereign cure had been
found for the chief political distempers of mankind.
Some, like Hallam, took their patriotism soberly. In
others it glowed with an ardent flame; but in all
patriotic sentiment was subordinate to ethical convictions. It was a tradition among the Whigs, established
by Burke, enriched by the eloquence of Sheridan
and Charles Lord Grey, that the early history of
the East India Company's rule had been defaced by
grave abuses. Macaulay was indoctrinated with this
view of Indian history and gave it the support of his
eloquence. How often at Holland House must he not
have heard the echoes of the most famous political
trial in recent history, when for some years the great
English pro-consul was confronted with the leaders
of the Whig party in a struggle which raised every

ethical problem in the government of an Oriental empire by a Western people. Lord Holland had received the story from the lips of his famous uncle and told Macaulay how, in the opinion of Charles James Fox, Sheridan's speech on the Oudh charge was the finest ever made in the House of Commons.

From the views entertained by the managers of the impeachment in 1787 Macaulay only partially liberated himself. The historian so far escaped from the tradition of the politicians as to acknowledge that Hastings had great qualities and had rendered remarkable services to the State. But he did not acquit him of grave faults, which a mind free of adverse prepossessions would either have failed to discover, or at least have greatly reduced, and of his friend Sir Elijah Impey he paints a picture which the true facts of the case do not even distantly justify.

But if the disposition of the Whig historians to find fault with their countrymen, when censure seemed to be deserved, led to some errors, on balance it has greatly served the public interest. The determination of the Whigs to uphold the cause of just and humane government at all times and in all circumstances and to tolerate no falling short of their ethical standard, on grounds of colour, race, or nationality, has had three important and wholly beneficial consequences. It has strengthened the integrity of English historical writing. It has prevented much practical evil. It has helped to inscribe the sense of trusteeship for the weaker races among the permanent conventions of the British Empire. The ethical view of the Empire preached by

Burke and Macaulay has become the enduring possession of British statesmanship.

Though there was a strength of conviction in the
Whig historians, amounting at certain sensitive points
to obstinate prejudice, there was a liberality in them
and a breadth of view far transcending the common
measure of their age. They made a real attempt to
understand alien peoples, some of them weak and distant and defenceless, and all of them unlike the
pleasant gentlemen who might be met in London
Clubs—Hindus and Moslems, negroes growing sugar
in Jamaica or cotton in the Southern States, litigious
New England democrats, Frenchmen shaken by the
revolutionary fever, even the down-trodden peasantry
in Connaught. Despite the palpable misconceptions
of the *Vindiciae Gallicae* there is vision in that youthful
tract of Mackintosh describing the valuable elements
in the French revolution and composed at a time when
neither the abuses of the Ancien Régime nor the great
advance in the science of government contained in the
early measures of the French Assembly were appreciated in England. Nor did Macaulay, stout Protestant as he was, and fully as he enters into the emotions
of the black Protestants who defended Londonderry,
blind himself to the claims of the Catholic peasantry of
Ireland. He defended the Maynooth Grants and
staked his Parliamentary career upon the concession
of educational facilities to the Irish Catholics. William
Napier, a Whig of the extreme left, carried both his
admiration for our French opponents and his contempt for our Spanish allies in the Peninsular War to

the point of extravagance, and on receiving the news
of Napoleon's death at St. Helena was overcome by
emotion for several hours. Napier combined with
military courage the gifts of an historian, the zeal of a
demagogue, and the temperament of a poet; but there
was more insight in his sense of the value for Spain of
Napoleonic ideas than can be found in most of the
British political literature of the period.

It was a note of these Whig writers to enjoy and
applaud the enviable qualities of the British aristocracy. They believed that public affairs were best
regulated when they were in the hands of the middle-
class, supported by the most enlightened members of
the aristocracy and the most prudent section of the
artisan population. No one of them was an academic
teacher. All of them had in one way or another procured two things very serviceable to success as an
historical writer, leisure, and either a direct share in
·public life or access to the society of governing people.
There is a grasp of reality in all their work which is
absent from many learned publications of the cloister.
Macaulay's account of the panic of 1692–5 is a case in
point. 'You will not', says Bagehot, 'find the cause of
panics so accurately explained in the dryest of political
economists—in the Scotch McCulloch.'[1]

In general the Whigs rejected the use of *a priori*
reasoning in politics; but there was one exception to
their general rule. They held the Austinian theory of
indivisible sovereignty to be an impregnable axiom of
political science. It follows that their predictions rest

[1] *Lit. Studies*, ii. 250.

either upon the experience of a pre-industrial age or else upon an axiom of politics which is now much shaken in authority. Macaulay thought that universal suffrage would be the end of civilization and could not conceive how, sovereignty being indivisible, the Empire could be kept together if colonial parliaments were accorded independence.

'If', he writes, 'the time comes when the mother country finds it expedient altogether to abdicate the paramount authority over a colony, one of two courses ought to be taken. There ought to be complete incorporation, if such incorporation be possible. If not, there ought to be complete separation. Very few propositions in politics can be so perfectly demonstrated as this, that Parliamentary government cannot be carried on by two really equal and independent parliaments in one Empire.'[1]

These Austinian doctrines are unequal to the subtlety of nature, and have been demonstrably falsified in the recent history of the British Commonwealth of Nations. The Whigs have no monopoly of prescience.

If, however, we hold the thesis that an historian is advantaged by the possession of strong political convictions and by an active interest in the political movements of his own age, then there is a strong case for the view that the type of political faith most likely to conduce to good historical writing is Whig rather than Tory or Radical. The Whigs occupied a central position. They sympathized with the aristocracy, they had close ties with the moneyed people, they were anxious to benefit the masses, and to make the name

[1] *History of England*, c. xxiii.

of English government synonymous with humanity and justice. A clergyman of genius, with some experience of an urban slum, could catch sides of the national life which were hidden from their view, for the new industrial underworld hardly entered into their horizon, and their minds were untouched by 'the torment of divine things'. But there was this advantage in the central position of the Whigs, that they were able to estimate from personal knowledge or family tradition all the factors in national life which had been up to 1832 associated with the government of the country. Had they been more extreme in the Tory or the Radical direction, they would have seen less and have had less to teach. Their histories have benefited by the golden mediocrity of their political views. Michelet, the revolutionary, was in some respects a greater historical genius than Macaulay, but, though more of a medievalist, he never knew his France as Macaulay knew his England.

In the Imperialist and Tory wave of recent years, the Whig tradition has been sharply challenged by a number of able historical writers, who sympathize with the royalists in the seventeenth, and with the Tories in the eighteenth century. Once a controversy always a controversy. The great debate between two schools of thought, the one inclining to authority, the other to liberty, the one disposed to the conservation of that which is old, the other to experimentation in that which is new, will continue as long as human nature remains unchanged. The genius of Macaulay has not estopped the critics. But then neither have the critics estopped the readers of Macaulay. Moreover, in the last resort, that school of historical interpretation will be most likely to prevail, in which men may rediscover the feelings by which they are themselves moved, the ideas which they themselves entertain, and the principles of action which they follow in their own lives or cherish and admire in the conduct of others.

Macaulay's persistent good fortune pursued him beyond the grave. He possessed a favourite nephew who shared his opinions, inherited many of his gifts, and with a rare depth of sympathy and manly tenderness interpreted him to the world in a biography which is one of the classics of English literature.

Sir George Otto Trevelyan, who died in August 1928 at the patriarchal age of ninety, was the son of an enlightened and progressive Indian administrator, and brought up in that generous tradition of public service and wide literary culture which is specially associated with the leading figures in Whig society during the later half of the eighteenth and earlier half of the nineteenth centuries. He was the inheritor of a large landed estate and married into a family enriched through their talents and energies by the process which is commonly described as the Industrial Revolution. When in 1897 he retired to his Northumbrian library he had served for thirty-two years in the House of Commons and had held five Government offices. His membership of Brooks' dated back to the days when the servants wore knee breeches and a small group of members would dine together sumptuously

three or four times a year and solemnly drink a toast
to the memory of Mr. Fox. Few men have been more
conversant with the social and political life of England
during the reign of George III, or had a keener relish
for the memorials of that age. At Harrow and Trinity,
Cambridge, he had learnt to admire the classical
authors whose writings formed the chief part of the
education of our ancestors. He loved the poems and
speeches which they loved and shared in their hearty
enjoyment of the sports and pleasures of English
country life. The Whig leaders of the eighteenth
century belonged to that well-to-do society of territorial magnates of which he was a member. The public
duties which they discharged from their homes in
the country or from their seats in Parliament were
familiar to him from long practice, and as he studied
the Parliamentary records in the days when Fox was
declaiming against the Government of Lord North,
he could appreciate and applaud fine points of strategy,
which would be likely to escape the student who had
never taken part in the strenuous work of a parliament. The landed and political class of that age
possessed many faults and foibles from which Sir
George Trevelyan was exempt, but of their characteristic virtues he had a full measure. So it pleased
him to note illustrations now of their simplicity, now
of their cultivation, such as a shooting party sped
from a country house for a long day among fields and
coverts with no lunch more substantial than bread and
cheese and a bag of onions, or a costly work of learning
such as Adam's treatise on the palace of Diocletian at

Spalato, financed mainly by the liberal contributions of men whose cheeks were rosy with claret and fresh country air.

Much of this knowledge and interest came to him in the most painless of all ways, through inheritance or family connexion or through the experience which young men of good family who enter political life cannot fail to acquire. 'For a student', he writes, 'whose estimate of beauty and charm in books is not regulated by the conventional values of the auction room, there is no inheritance more desirable than a library collected by ancestors who read and travelled during the middle portion of the eighteenth century.'[1] Such a library, containing Macaulay's books vigorously annotated by the great historian, Sir George had inherited. There were books in that library of the purest Whig descent. 'The volumes of the Gentleman's Magazine', he writes, 'used for this History (*The History of the American Revolution*) belonged to one who knew the truth about Long Island, for they contain the bookplate of Marquis Cornwallis. The set was purchased by Macaulay so that the well-thumbed pages have never passed out of Whig hands.'[2]

Apart from his delightful biography of his uncle and a poignant little piece on Cawnpore, Sir George's contributions to historical learning belong to that period of our national history when the fox-hunting aristocracy of England, whose social position was never before so enviable, or their virtues and vices so

[1] *George III and Charles Fox*, vol. i, p. 54.
[2] *American Revolution*, vol. ii, p. 291.

important for the world, were first confronted with the strange problem of new empires beyond the Indian and Atlantic oceans. In the famous opening chapter of his *History of England* Macaulay had set against the great historic achievements of the English people 'great national crimes or follies far more humiliating than any disaster', and of these he gives two instances, the policy which led to the loss of the American colonies and the failure of England to find a tolerable solution of the Irish problem. As Irish Secretary in the dark days following the murder of Lord Frederick Cavendish, Sir George Trevelyan had the best reasons for knowing how little progress had been made on the path of Anglo-Irish reconciliation. But the other great crime and folly had worked itself out to an issue. The American colonies had been lost and would never be recovered. The circumstances under which they were lost, the origins and course of the dispute had been made the subject of continuous investigation in the United States and supplied, until the outbreak of the War of Secession furnished a new topic, the grandest and most inviting theme upon which an American historian could deploy his talent. The results were only what might have been anticipated. The early American historians of the quarrel, writing while the natural resentments caused by the war were still living memories, dealt in very bright lights and very deep shadows. They depicted Britain as the oppressor, the colonies as innocent and self-respecting victims. In British policy they saw nothing but a tissue of follies and crimes; and in the act by which the

colonies declared their Independence the most fortunate achievement of the British race. In the course
of two generations a great body of historical doctrine
was built up, the effect of which was indelibly to im-
print upon the mind of every school-child in the
United States the idea of Great Britain as the traditional enemy of American freedom.

As a staunch Whig Sir George Trevelyan did not
dispute the thesis of these earlier American historians.
In common with Bancroft and others he regarded the
American policy of George III and his ministers as
foolish to the point of criminality. He was not even
disposed to allow to George Grenville, who introduced the Stamp Tax, the benefit of such alleviating
circumstances as are conceded by G. L. Beer, that
admirable American student of the period, who points
out that the Seven Years War had practically doubled
the National Debt, that the colonies had already (1754)
shown their unwillingness to unite, that the old system
under which troops were requisitioned had proved
unworkable, that Grenville's object was to use the
colonial revenue solely for the purpose of providing
the colonies with military defence, and that his scheme
was only calculated to yield an income sufficient to
meet from one-third to somewhat less than one-half
of the cost of the American army.[1] In this respect Sir
George may perhaps be regarded as more American

[1] G. L. Beer, *British Colonial Policy*. See also E. I. McCormac,
*Colonial Opposition to Imperial Authority during the French and
Indian Wars*, C. H. Van Tyne, *Causes of the War of Independence*,
and H. L. Osgood, *The American Colonies in the Eighteenth Century*.

than that later school of American historians who
have imbibed the canons of strict impartiality in the
Faculties of their native universities. The question
whether a good theoretical case could or could not
be stated for Grenville's taxes is in his view a minor
matter. However well-intentioned the taxes may have
been, they showed themselves from the first to be
violently unpopular. The most ordinary prudence
counselled their immediate abandonment and the
surrender of any project to obtain supplies from the
colonies other than those which might be freely voted
by the Colonial Assemblies.

Accordingly the fiscal controversy does not with Sir
George fill more than a small portion of the landscape.
In a series of seven delightful volumes, the *Early Years
of Charles James Fox*, the *American Revolution*, and
George III and Charles Fox, Sir George sets himself
down to portray English and American life and politics
during the generation which witnessed the fatal dis-
ruption of the two branches of the English-speaking
race. If Fox is the principal figure on the English side,
it was because Fox found his political soul in those
anxious and gloomy days when he led the national
opposition to the war policy of George III and his
Prime Minister Lord North; but Sir George does not
begin his story with the Stamp Act. His first volume,
entitled the *Early History of Charles James Fox*, published in 1880, was devoted to a study of the social
and political life of the ruling classes in England in the
late sixties and early seventies of the eighteenth century. To understand the American revolution, it is

necessary to know something of the tone and temper
of the political aristocracy in Britain, who at the critical
moment in the development of English civilization
had the deciding word. The old Puritan fervour had
died away, the new era of political principle, firmly
and indeed passionately held, had not yet dawned.
The early years of Charles James Fox were lived at a
time when the fibre of our public men had grown
dangerously lax, when 'the stern heroes who waged
the great civic contest of the seventeenth century and
who drew their strength from the highest of all sources
had been succeeded by a race who in private very
generally lived for enjoyment and in Parliament fought
for their own hand'. Of this brilliant, pleasure-loving
society, sensitive to the allurements of the new wealth
which was pouring in from India, and caring little
or nothing for the deeper concerns of the national
life, Sir George has drawn a brilliant picture. From
the first scene of the drama the *dénouement* may be
predicted; for something wider than the Atlantic
separates the Rigbys and Bedfords from the Puritan
colonists of New England.

Now this temporary relaxation of fibre in the public
men of a country is apt to occur in the years immediately succeeding a great struggle, when the great
achievement is in the recent past, and no fresh issue
has arisen capable of firing the imagination, and
politics seem to be empty of everything but personal
rivalries. That is the dangerous period, the period of
political infidelities during which irretrievable mis-
takes are often made. Such a relaxation of political

fibre occurred in the United States after the close of the war between North and South, and it occurred in England after the close of the Seven Years War.

The effect of this demoralization in the governing class has been very well brought out by Sir George Trevelyan. It enabled the King, who was an honest, steadfast, laborious man, with a high sense of duty and a great conception of his office, to control Cabinet and Parliament and to impose his own policy on the country. The American War was primarily the King's war. Even Lord North, the King's Prime Minister, had abandoned all belief in it long before the Peace came. It was the King who managed year after year to defeat an Opposition, over-languid at first but steadily gaining strength until, after twelve years of the North administration, it was able to convert itself into a Government.

Another feature of the situation which receives a good deal of attention from Sir George is the extent of the opposition to the war in England. The three greatest statesmen of the country—Chatham, Burke, and Fox—were all against it. The younger Pitt, who came into Parliament during its concluding phase, declared his firm opposition. All four members for the City of London voted steadily against the war from start to finish. The leading London newspaper was pro-American or anti-war. When Lord Effingham threw up his commission rather than serve against the colonists and declared in the House of Lords that, when the duties of a soldier and a citizen became inconsistent, he should always think himself obliged to

sink the character of a soldier in that of a citizen, the
corporations of London and Dublin voted him their
public thanks. The case of Lord Effingham does not
stand alone. Augustus Keppel, Vice-Admiral of the
White, and Sir Jeffery Amherst, probably the first
soldier in the kingdom, flatly refused to serve against
the Americans, and their example was followed by
not a few officers of every rank. That naval and
military officers should sacrifice their professional
prospects in this way is remarkable enough. It is even
more symptomatic of the temper of the times that
they do not seem to have suffered in the estimation
of their contemporaries by dissociating themselves
in so marked a way from a war in which the military
and naval forces of the Crown were engaged. Such
examples justify the historian's verdict that the 'American war from onset to finish was an open question in
English society'.

From these premisses the conclusion naturally follows that the American quarrel is not so much with
England as with the King and that comparatively
small circle of political adherents through whom the
King worked his policy in the Cabinet and in Parliament. Samuel Curwen, a Massachusetts loyalist,
reported that most of the middle classes throughout
the kingdom were American. His verdict is in sub-
stance confirmed by John Wesley, whose travels on
horseback through every part of the country gave
him an incomparable opportunity of testing the real
opinion of the English people. Writing of a memo-
randum which Wesley addressed to Lord North, in

which the facts about the public attitude to the American war are set out, Sir George comments as follows: 'It is impossible to read that plain and forcible statement without reflecting on the lamentable fact that the middle class of citizens to which Wesley belonged was to all intents and purposes excluded from the higher administration of the country.'[1]

The fact that the majority, or, if not the majority, a considerable section of the British people, were opposed to the attempt to coerce the colonies had not been generally appreciated by the United States. The admirable and judicious observations of Lecky, being comprised in a *History of England*, had been chiefly noticed by the English public; but the significance of the evidence marshalled in Trevelyan's *American Revolution* could hardly be missed on the other side of the Atlantic. 'It would not be easy', wrote a contributor to a well-known New York journal, 'to estimate the effect which such a demonstration ought to have and doubtless will have on the feeling with which Americans will hereafter regard Great Britain. It is manifest that most of the school histories on the United States will have to be re-written.'

Historical legends die hard, and we have recently learned from Professor Van Tyne[2] that in the Middle West of America, where the Irish and German elements are strong, the adherents of the old anti-British tradition of historical writing maintain a strong rear-

[1] *American Revolution*, vol. ii, p. 47.
[2] C. H. Van Tyne, *England and America*.

guard action against the new forces of academic impartiality. One proposition, however, even the advocates of the Yellow Press will not contest. The Irish and Germans who now form so important an element in the population of the Middle West were a negligible factor in the old colonies which made the American revolution. There were probably, says Sir George Trevelyan, not three hundred real Celts in the continental line, and the rest of the Irish were emigrants and the children of emigrants from Protestant Ulster. The revolution was an English act made by Englishmen acting upon English principles, influenced by English traditions, and sharing to the full the prejudices of Protestant England. In Massachusetts, the centre of the revolt, the Quebec Act which granted toleration to the French Catholics was 'as unpopular as the Boston Port Act itself'.

It is this essential English character of the American revolution against the fruits of the system of personal government which Sir George Trevelyan had been so successful in bringing before the imagination of his readers. He regards the American rebels as Englishmen whose effectual protest against the methods of despotism on American soil led to the protection and subsequent enlargement of our island liberties. If in many respects they were narrow in their vision, so too were the Puritans of the Long Parliament. If they objected to standing armies and taxation without representation, so too did the Whigs on our side of the Atlantic. If their sense of individual liberty was stronger than their appreciation of the needs of the

State, this was only to be expected of an English democracy living under the free and rough conditions of colonial life. The great figure of Washington is essentially British.

It is also worthy of observation that though there were many circumstances in the war calculated to provoke the extreme of ill-feeling, notably the employment on the British side of Red Indians and of German mercenaries whose standards and ideas were different from those which prevailed in the British army, there was, outside the distant regions of Georgia and Carolina, little of calculated atrocity. 'All over the States of Pennsylvania and New Jersey and New York throughout New England,' writes Sir George, 'there was neither shooting nor hanging of prisoners taken in battle. The revolutionary war afforded in this respect a marked contrast to the treatment of the Jacobites after Culloden and of the Irish insurgents after the rebellion of ninety-eight.'[1] The worst exception to this observation, the disgraceful murder of the garrison of Fort Griswold near New Haven after they had laid down their arms, must be put to the account of a band of American loyalists under the command of Benedict Arnold.

The dark story of the war is relieved by many pleasant instances of chivalrous behaviour on either side. In its advance southward General Burgoyne's army had been accompanied by a horde of Indians whose cruelties the British officer in command was totally unable to restrain. Yet when the British forces

[1] *American Revolution*, vol. iv, p. 258.

capitulated at Saratoga they were treated with a generous consideration by the American commanders, which illustrates the essential humanity of the English combatants on either side. Despite the fact that the British general had burned down General Schuyler's fine house at Saratoga, he was received as an honoured guest, introduced to Mrs. Schuyler and her family, and entertained at the Schuyler house in Albany with 'every demonstration of hospitality'. The Congressmen were less honourable than the generals. The Convention of Saratoga, under which General Burgoyne laid down his arms, was repudiated on the flimsiest pretexts as too favourable to the British. This act, as Sir George observes, is a blot on the lustre of the American revolution. It is no real defence to contend that in coming to a compact with their enemy in the field the American generals exceeded their powers.

The amazing lack of practical imagination which characterized the American policy of George III was also evidenced in the conduct of the war. The British troops were clad without reference to the character and the vicissitudes of the climate in which they were to operate. Opposed to a body of skilled riflemen, who made it their special object to mark down the officers of the contending force, they made no effort to improve their shooting but continued to put their faith in the bayonet which had served them well in European wars. But the crowning stupidity was the absence of strict discipline in Lord Howe's army. The population of the American colonies was by no means united in feeling on the question of the war. Tom Paine came to America a few months after the breaking-out of hostilities. 'I found', he said, 'the disposition such that they might have been led by a thread and governed by a reed. Their suspicion was quick and penetrating, but their attachment to Britain was obstinate and it was at that time a kind of treason to speak against it.' Paine is, perhaps, not altogether to be trusted, for there were others beside Samuel Adams who from the first were resolutely working for independence. But even in Massachusetts, where this feeling was strongest, there were many loyalists, and it is noticeable that Washington was never able to collect an army of more than 20,000. The exercise of the commonest prudence enjoined that the utmost pains should be taken to conciliate those colonists who still remained loyal to the British connexion. Their property should have been scrupulously respected and their help enlisted in the task of civil government in those areas in which a British predominance had been established. Nothing of this was done. The army of Lord Howe pillaged the homes of loyalist and rebel with indiscriminating vigour. Nothing was sacred from their greed, neither the libraries in Princetown and New York, nor even the mathematical and scientific instruments in the seats of learning, nor the quiet loyalist homesteads in New Jersey or New York State. After the loyalist troops had been at work for three weeks in the county of West Chester, 'the people though untouched in life and limb were as utterly denuded and impoverished as if an invasion of Iroquois and Seneca warriors had swept the country'. And so far from enlisting loyalists in the task of civil government, no civil government was ever set up even in New York. We can hardly wonder that the recruitment of loyalist volunteers languished and that there were no more than 2,500 loyalists enlisted in the British forces.

When we consider that the last six volumes of this spirited book were composed between the ages of sixty and seventy-six, by an author who had behind him a long and strenuous Parliamentary career, we shall not expect them to embody all the latest refinements of Transatlantic research. Those accomplished historians J. A. Doyle and F. J. Turner have pointed to some errors and omissions. The learning is indeed considerable and discursive, and the gift of narrative conspicuously brilliant; but in a work of this kind destined to affect the view which two great societies will in future entertain of a deep historical controversy, in which they have taken opposite parts and which has left a long legacy of bitterness behind it, there is something as valuable as learning and more to be prized than literary elegance, and that is a large charity of judgement. It is in this quality that the peculiar excellence of the work of Sir George Trevelyan's later years is to be found. There can be few military histories more impartial, and the reader who did not already know Sir George's nationality would find some difficulty in guessing it, as he follows his eloquent guide in the train of the contending armies.

The schools of scientific history which have lately sprung up in our universities have done much to raise the standard of historical scholarship in this country. But what university professor would dare to issue a book so full of pleasant excursions and little caprices, so clearly written to gratify the author's personal taste and interest and so faintly affected by the rigours of the game as Trevelyan's *American Revolution*? The Histories of Macaulay and his nephew could not have been produced from university chairs. There is something unacademic in their impetuous flood of entertaining detail. We miss the deadly relevance and cold impartiality of the seminar. But so long as a taste for good letters survives among those who use our English tongue, the reader in search of enjoyment will never resort in vain to the two Whig kinsmen who have transmitted to posterity in a vestment of fresh and glowing colours one of the governing traditions of English public life.

IV

AMERICA AFTER FIFTEEN YEARS[1]

1909–24

IT is fifteen years since I last visited the United States. A short time, maybe, if measured by seconds, minutes, and hours, but long enough if we take account of the great changes which have transformed the political landscape of the world during this crowded and momentous period. For consider just a few of the happenings of these stirring fifteen years—the revolution in China, perhaps the most complete revolution in all history, the Great War, the downfall of the three European empires, the resurrection of Poland, the establishment of a Communist government in Russia, the dictatorship of Mussolini in Italy, the abolition of the Khalifat, the grant of autonomy to Catholic Ireland and of practical self-government to the three hundred and twenty-two million inhabitants of the Indian continent. A very crowded fifteen years! More than a century of change seems to have been packed into them.

What, however, of the United States? Has this great, conservative empire, so wealthy, so fortunately remote from the central storm-centre of world politics, so absorbed in its own business and pleasures, also undergone changes? Are there any alterations of mentality discernible to the close observer? Any change in the trend and working of institutions? Any

[1] Reprinted from *Scribner's Magazine*, vol. lxxvii, no. 4.

new tokens of revolt and impatience? Any transformations in the constitution and customs of American society? Those are the questions which, visiting
America after this interval of fifteen years, I naturally
put to myself.

The first, the most obvious, and the most enduring
impression which I have derived from my visit is that
of a great advance in the diffusion of material prosperity and comfort.

Fifteen years ago America was a very rich country.
She is far richer now, richer absolutely and richer by
comparison with the rest of the world. There has
never been in the whole course of history a society
in which the means of material comfort were so widely
or amply diffused as they are in the America of to-day.
In England cabinet ministers cannot afford to keep
motor-cars. In America, thanks in the main to the
enterprise of Mr. Henry Ford, a car is regarded as a
perquisite essential to the normal working household.
Professors and students, typists and bricklayers, the
humblest operative as well as the wealthiest millionaire own, or appear to own, a car. Little children
drive about in toy automobiles. In Los Angeles there
is a car to every four persons, children included.
When winter comes the roads of Florida are black not
only with the automobiles of the wealthy in search of
change and sunshine, but also with the Ford cars of
the working-men. American civilization is on wheels.
There are few problems which engage more attention
than that of parking, and how beautifully developed
the art of parking has become! With what neatness

and dexterity is the machine manœuvred into its
appointed niche within four inches from the pave-
ment! For every one appears to be able to drive in
America. It has become one of the national arts, as
widely diffused as the taste for music in Germany,
or dramatic appreciation among the ancient Greeks.
Indeed, one of the arguments advanced in favour of
prohibition is that in a society in which most citizens
are engine-drivers drunkenness is not a private vice
but a public danger. This great development has
sprung up in the last decade. Fifteen years ago no
one asked himself the question whether he could get
about quicker on foot than in a car in one of your
great cities. Now that question is frequently asked
and the answer, as often as not, comes down on the
side of the pedestrian. By a curious irony the demand
for speedy motion, if carried beyond a certain point,
defeats its own end. Out of overmuch mobility there
results immobility. The luxury of the few, becoming
the necessity of the many, ceases to yield the old
revenue of pleasure. There will come a time, and
that not very far distant, when cars will be so numerous
that half the enjoyment of using them will disappear.
Meanwhile the whole American people is rioting in
this new source of power over place and time.

Then there is the radio. Fifteen years ago we had
not heard of the radio. Now every tenement-house
in New York is fitted up with a wireless apparatus.
The listeners-in have become a powerful factor in
politics, the more powerful inasmuch as no one
knows, or from the nature of the case can know, with

certainty what effect listening-in does in point of fact exert. I have heard it said that the last presidential election was determined by the 'radio mind', that the 'listeners-in' being immune from the temperamental excitement which is generated by a great meeting, conceived a disgust at the extravagance of the Democratic Convention and determined to vote Republican by way of protest. I cannot believe this. The result of the presidential election is capable of a very much broader explanation. America said to herself, 'We are very prosperous as we are, why change?' The mammoth plurality of Mr. Coolidge requires no further diagnosis.

Still it would be idle to deny to this new and wonderful invention great potentialities of influence in the future. The listener-in forms his own judgement in the quiet atmosphere of his own home. His verdict, therefore, is likely to be less emotional than that of the frequenter of public meetings; the 'psychology of the crowd' has less influence; prose counts for more; poetry weighs lighter in the balance. One might expect then that the listening-in habit will tend to reduce the value of mere oratory and to strengthen the reflective elements in the public opinion of the nation. If so, its influence will be all to the good.

An extraordinary development of motion-pictures is also a feature of the history of this period. Los Angeles has grown great and illustrious on the films. The motion-picture is indeed a peculiarly American form of art. Other nations dabble in it, America pursues it with passionate intensity and spreads its film fashions and the fame and features of its 'film stars' throughout the world. As an inexpensive means of providing amusement, combined with a little instruction, to a vast population, much of it imperfectly equipped with a knowledge of the language of the country, the motion-picture plays a useful role. For such a public, tragedy is too august, comedy too nimble, farce too idiomatic, music too profound. The motion-picture, with a minimum of audible sounds, makes an appeal to the eye as intelligible to the latest immigrant from Lodz or Aleppo as to the scion of the oldest colonial family in Virginia or Massachusetts.

I place in the forefront these three important inventions because they are helping the American nation to solve one of the gravest problems which confront an industrial democracy when once it has reached a certain level of material prosperity. How is it to dispose of its leisure time? A hundred years ago that was a comparatively unimportant question in America. Even fifteen years ago it was a great deal less important than it is now. It was less important because there was less leisure and less surplus wealth. Now it has become all-important. The American democracy has become possessed of leisure and of money; and within the last fifteen years science has come to its help and whispered in tones of apparently irresistible fascination, 'Drive cars, enjoy the movies, listen in'.

The organization of popular amusements is a great and necessary part of the social art. No wise man will despise it. You in America have always been an open-air people. You were a people of farmers long before you had begun to develop your factories and, now that you have developed a great industrial population, you have begun again to take to the road and the open air. I confess that I am amazed at the scale and rapidity of your athletic developments. You were thinking a great deal about football fifteen years ago, for did I not see the Harvard stadium crowded for the annual match between Harvard and Yale, and for at least a month before that great event feed as part of my daily intellectual diet upon the vaticinations of the daily press as to the relative form of the contending teams? But there have been immense developments in the football world since then. Here is an incident which certainly impresses the foreign visitor. There was a match quite recently between the Universities of Wisconsin and Illinois in the stadium at Urbana. The stadium at Urbana, be it observed, is constructed to hold sixty-seven thousand spectators (I wonder what Abraham Lincoln, who used to do justice in a little court-house near by, would have thought of this) and was erected by the patriotic zeal of the alumni of the university. On that great day a stream of special trains ran out from Chicago at intervals of fifteen minutes to the scene of the encounter, the first train starting at 6 a.m., the last returning at 2 o'clock the next morning, and conveyed to and fro thirty thousand enthusiasts from that great city. Thirty thousand human beings willing to travel eight hours by train for a football match! What a diffusion of athletic interest through the community is implied by such a transaction!

Golf has come in with a vengeance. Fifteen years

ago it was practically unknown. Now it is universal and practised by old and young alike of either sex with inflexible pertinacity and ardour. The business man, relaxing the stoical pursuit of dollars to the brink of the grave, and having made his sufficiency, now bends his will to the improvement of his game on the links. First he tries to break a hundred, then to break ninety, and then, if he proves to have skill, to get round in seventy-six. The country clubs are fitted with every luxury, the greens are carefully watered, a new and very effective grass has been discovered, and no pains are spared to make the links as good as science and money can make them.

All this is, of course, very expensive. Golf is in the main a rich man's game, but not altogether. There is a nine-hole municipal course on the outskirts of Buffalo, hard by the gleaming waters of Niagara, upon which the factory hands play in their hundreds of an evening when released from industrial toil. All this constitutes an immense change. A new *lingua franca* has been created for the whole continent. Wherever you travel, from the Atlantic shore to the Pacific coast, from the Canadian border to the Gulf of Mexico —there is one almost unfailing bond of common interest—the ancient and royal game of golf.

America has not yet become a country of book-lovers. For one traveller consuming a book in a railway-car you will find a hundred occupied with magazines or newspapers—more particularly with newspapers. American journalism was somewhat of a portent to a European traveller fifteen years ago, for you realized sooner than did our newspaper men in the old country the huge new public for the printed word which the primary schools in an industrial democracy were creating, and the kind of intellectual or non-intellectual food which that public demanded. But many of your methods have now been adopted for better or worse in the old country, and your newspaper is therefore not quite so great a shock to us as it was. It has, however, developed in two quite distinct directions, one of which seems to me to be bad and the other good, in recent years. The daily paper has swollen beyond all recognition in size. On week-days it is a formidable armful. On Sundays it is a whole library. There cannot be a single day in the year in which the New York *Times* does not print more words than are contained in the Gospels, or a Sunday on which it is not more verbose than the Old Testament. In these amazing miscellanies every want is supplied except that of a sustained and continuous interest. Fashions, athletics, novelettes, art and politics, social scandals, crimes and divorces, anecdotes and intimacies, any little detail which can flick the jaded curiosity of the idler, above all tons of local gossip, are collected by some powerful machine and discharged with diurnal punctuality at the head of the American citizen. It is amazing how he bears up under the load, how making a long voyage he buys the papers of one zone after another as the newsvendor invades the car and obtrudes them on his attention. The American newspaper, a thing in the main of deftly chosen scraps and patches, is like the cinematograph and responds to the same craving. It offers not food for reflection, but a vast canvas of miscellaneous word-pictures, imposed upon a huge scaffolding of lucrative advertisements. Here there is no perspective, no accentuation of the important issues, no careful differentiation of the transactions of the day according to any standard of intrinsic significance. It is easy to see that the high lights and the low lights upon the theatre have not been arranged by Clio, the muse of history. But what matters? Newspapers are made to sell, as razors are made to cut, and, judged by this test, American journalism is a brilliant success. Fifty-five million papers are sold every day to an eager and impatient public.

The growth in the sheer bulk and volume of the more important newspapers must not be misinterpreted. It is not, unless I greatly err, the result of a growing appetite for reading among the American public. Nor is it the fruit of an enlarged intellectual curiosity. Indeed, the explanation is not to be found in the intellectual sphere at all. The phenomenon is purely commercial and serves as an additional illustration of that surprising increment of material prosperity to which I have already drawn attention. The newspapers have swollen because the advertisements have increased and for no other reason. A sufficient powder of literary material must be sprinkled over the illimitable table-land of commercial jam.

I cannot think that in thus swelling out its dimensions the newspaper press has added to its intellectual usefulness, however serviceable this process may incidentally be to the dissemination of knowledge as to saleable commodities. There is, however, another direction, and that of the utmost importance, in which the press of America has made clear and evident progress during the past fifteen years. There are many American papers to-day which are awake to the outside world.

This was not the case fifteen years ago. At that time it was impossible to follow with intelligence the course of world events in the American daily press. Occasionally there would be a shaft of light upon a particular topic, but then in the most tantalizing way darkness supervened and a month might elapse before the subject was again referred to. There was no continuous supply of information from abroad. There was no continuous commentary upon world affairs. It was impossible for any American reader, however desirous he might be to inform himself, to obtain from the daily press any just appreciation of the general situation of politics. A divorce, a murder, a sensational case of graft, the death or illness of an important public character—were quite sufficient to divert or to arrest or even to dry up the most promising flow of information upon the most important themes in the region of foreign affairs.

I notice a great change now. An artist might symbolize it by a fresco depicting the giant figure of America, the symbols of material wealth thickly strewn around her couch, slowly waking up to the world. In several American newspapers—it would perhaps be invidious to particularize—it is possible to find news which is both careful and well selected as to the happenings in foreign lands. Some papers are more adventurous and make a definite effort to direct the public judgement. Moreover, the New York *Times*, which has perhaps gone farther than any other organ in the direction of disseminating foreign news and accompanying it with an appropriate commentary, has come—thanks to the air mail—to exert an influence all over the Union and not merely in the Eastern States. There are many households in which this excellent paper figures as the second organ, read in the evening or a day late, while the local newspaper is read at the breakfast-table.

Moreover, for the more serious student there is now an admirable periodical entitled *Foreign Affairs*, edited by Professor Archie Coolidge of Harvard University. Add to this the numerous clubs for international affairs, the special 'World-Mind' alcoves in public libraries, the summer school at Williamstown, which attracts distinguished publicists from every country, and it will be seen that the thinking part of the American public is by no means content with an attitude of indifference to the larger movements of the world. It is true, indeed, that these interests have not as yet sunk very deep or spread very wide. The great mass of the population is still mainly and almost exclusively concerned with its own immediate interests. Nevertheless, there are clear signs of a change. New tendencies are at work. There is a discernible enlargement in the field of vision, and a certain weakening of the time-honoured bastions of American self-sufficiency.

Such a change might naturally be expected to result from the slow but certain growth of culture and knowledge; but it has, of course, been accelerated by America's entry into the War. Now the War has not exercised the great moral effects in America with which we in Great Britain are familiar. The country was not in it long enough. The sacrifices were by comparison slight. Australia, for instance, with only five million inhabitants, lost more men in killed than the whole of the United States. Only in Princeton—where the fine eagerness to engage was matched by a lamentable loss of life—was I conscious of the War as exercising a continuing influence over the genius of the place. But the War has at any rate stirred up an interest in general politics which did not previously exist. The young men in the universities are curious about Europe. Moreover, they have conceived a respect for Great Britain. The feeling towards my country is unquestionably more friendly than it was fifteen years ago. This I attribute to our recent confraternity in arms and also in part to the Irish settlement and the funding of the War debt.

Nevertheless, it is clear that America does not propose at present to enter the League of Nations. You are a very prosperous and therefore a very conservative nation, ready to scrap anything except political ideas. 'We are well enough as we are, why should we change?' is the thought which naturally occurs to the citizen reflecting on an expanding balance at the bank. So the great political maxims of the late eighteenth and early nineteenth century, the Monroe Doctrine, the doctrine of non-intervention, still retain their empire on the public mind. They are regarded as faithful servants not lightly to be dismissed.

Moreover, the League of Nations question has become fatally interwoven with party politics. To the hard-shelled Republican the League is Mr. Wilson's League and therefore abominable. If Mr. Wilson had wished to get his League accepted he should have taken the Republican 'reservations', but he was obstinate, and now even the acceptance of the reservations will fail to reconcile the party to the League. The Republican does not argue the League on its merits. It is sufficient for him that it bears marks of a Wilsonian origin. All the Republican leaders, the late Senator Lodge included, were League men before Mr. Wilson became a convert to the idea. But Mr. Wilson's imperious handling of the question alienated them. Strong party feelings swept them away from their moorings, and a very violent gale of public opinion will be needed to sweep them back.

Such gales or blizzards are not unknown in America, and occasionally hurtle with devastating force through the golden orchards of worldly-wise content. The passage of the Eighteenth Amendment to the Constitution, prohibiting the sale of intoxicants, was the result of such a blizzard. A tempest suddenly rose in the Protestant churches which swept the politicians in Washington off their feet. What has happened once may happen again. If the ministers of religion bestir themselves, if the women in America take up the League as they do in England as our one and only

shield and preservative against war, then America is
bound to come in. The reasons which are so easily
multiplied against participation, as, for instance, that
the covenant is badly drawn, that it involves incon-
venient commitments, that Japan is a member and
raises awkward questions, that America must consider her foreign populations, that the British domi-
nions are represented in the assembly, that the League
is too strong, or again that the League is too weak—
all these reasons will fall away and be replaced by
reasons equally cogent on the other side. At present,
however, the League is so unpopular that even Mr.
Davis was afraid to blazon it on his banner. He under-
took to refer it to a plebiscite.

This anti-League feeling must not, however, be
construed as indicating a simple return to the old
spirit of isolation. The War has generated a great and
unmistakable interest in world affairs among the
leaders of American intelligence. Nothing impressed
me more than the eagerness with which I was in-
terrogated by my friends and acquaintances in the
Eastern States with respect to the course of European
policy and more particularly of British party struggles.
Fifteen years ago there was far less interest and far less
knowledge. Now there is not only interest and knowledge but a desire to make America's weight felt in the
balances of world policy, provided only that this
should not be done through the instrumentality of the
League. Disarmament conferences by all means, so
long as they are summoned by the President of the
United States and not by the Council of the League,

and sit at Washington, not at Geneva. Americans in the League Secretariat, in the League Commissions, by all means, so long as they are not official representatives of the government but act in a private capacity. Let war be outlawed, so long as the enforcement of the decree of outlawry be not entrusted to the League of Nations, which has been constructed for the purpose. The good Republican, in fact, is anxious to do his duty to the world, but does not want to be shown the way by Mr. Wilson.

I do not deny that there is an influential body of men standing quite apart from the professional politicians who deplore America's abstention from the League, and are anxious that she should take up her membership. These are the university intellectuals. In the American seats of learning men are apt to view the situation very much as it is regarded in my own country. They say in effect: 'The League is by no means perfect, but it is doing good work for peace and conciliation and the promotion of humane causes. Moreover, it is the only permanent instrument constructed to this end. Therefore it ought to be supported.' These views, it is true, are held at present by a comparatively narrow circle. My impression, however, is that the personal eminence of the men who hold League opinions will by degrees secure for them a larger audience.

The political enfranchisement of women is so recent that it is impossible to forecast its future consequences for American life. It may, however, be noted that this was the first presidential election in which families were divided in political allegiance. Not that the women tended to vote one ticket rather than another, but that they were disposed to vote according to their inclinations and that these in some cases differed from those of the male members of the family. In one home with which I am acquainted the father voted for Mr. Coolidge, the mother for Mr. Davis, and the daughter for Mr. La Follette. It may be added that notwithstanding these variances complete harmony and good humour prevailed.

If the American women have not taken up the League of Nations as a distinctively woman's cause, they show abundant evidence of a growing concern in public welfare. Fifteen years ago the political self-consciousness of the American woman was a young, rare, and tender plant. Now it is robust and plentifully evident. Women's conferences, women's clubs, women's leagues, women's organizations for other than purely social purpose are greatly multiplied.

How far feminine influence operated in procuring the passage of the Eighteenth Amendment I cannot say, but those who contend that prohibition has come to stay in America are justified in pointing to the woman's vote as a factor likely to operate in favour of its continuance. Needless to say, no change which has come over America in recent years is more continually and ardently discussed than this daring piece of social legislation. By some it is vehemently denounced as a breach of the Constitution, as an intolerable interference with individual liberty, as the prolific parent of lawlessness and crime; by others it is defended as a heroic and successful remedy for a deep-seated social evil.

I am disposed to think that the world is not yet in a position to form an accurate estimate of the results for good and evil of this remarkable and audacious experiment. That it has been productive of serious evils is incontestable. The law is very widely evaded and more particularly by that class of society to whom the state most naturally looks for an example in the strict maintenance of law. It is said, and the statement is not seriously challenged, that anybody can get a drink who knows how, provided, however, that he is careless of price and quality. In the maritime cities the Americans are resisting the revenue laws now, just as they fought against them in the decades which preceded the Revolution. Only there is this difference: the old laws were imposed by a government in London; the new law is the work of the American democracy itself.

These are grave and incontestable evils. Every American lawyer and statesman deplores them. Nothing can be worse for the morale of a country than a widespread disregard of the law. Already Americans complain of the terrible prevalence of serious crime in their country, and of the great difficulty in securing convictions for murder. And now with prohibition, the forces making for lawless action and a cynical disregard for legality are enormously increased. When a firm impudently describes itself as 'official bootlegger to the Cabinet and the Supreme Court', it would be idle to deny the magnitude of the evil.

On the other hand, it is contended that far less liquor is drunk in the States under prohibition than was formerly consumed. I imagine that this is unquestionably true. Though the rich people who want liquor can obtain it at a price, the same facilities are not open to the poor. Employers of labour tell us that labour is more regular in consequence of prohibition, and that the industrial output of the country has been materially increased. Moreover, a saloon which operates in a back room and is liable to a police raid offers fewer temptations to the ordinary passer-by than a saloon flaunting its wares in the full light of day.

My belief is that the continuance of the Eighteenth Amendment will ultimately depend upon the extent to which the manufacturers can prove that the amendment is good for trade. As yet we have no figures which enable us to reach a conclusion. If, however, the American public becomes convinced that the new law has added to the industrial output of the country by abolishing drunkenness among the workers, then I cannot imagine that the decision will be reversed by reason of the fact, deplorable as it may be, that the rich can, by taking a little trouble, supply themselves with alcoholic refreshment at a high price. It is by its dollar-earning power that prohibition will eventually be judged. At present there is some reason to think that it may be good for business and calculated to strengthen America's competing power in the markets of the world. So long as this opinion prevails among hard-shelled 'economic men', the temperance idealists have auxiliaries powerful enough to enable

them to maintain the position. The experiment, however, is far too new to enable us to pronounce with
confidence as to its effects upon industry.

The Eighteenth Amendment was, I imagine, a great
triumph of social and religious idealism. It is also
illustrative of a tendency in American political thought
which may have been latent fifteen years ago, but
was certainly not obvious to the traveller's eye. I
allude to the growing disposition to regard the sacred
fabric of the Constitution as admitting of improvements.

Fifteen years ago I was told on all hands how very
difficult it was to alter the Constitution, and how
unlikely it was that serious changes would be made in
view of the exacting requirements of the Constitution.
Now it seems to me that the American people are
beginning to view the masterpiece of the Philadelphia
Convention with diminished reverence. Have you
not in recent years carried without apparent difficulty
three important amendments, and is not a fourth
under consideration as I write these words? Shade
of Madison! The day may even come when America
will say of the house which you designed for her, that
in this age of steam and electricity it would be the
better for considerable improvements.

V

A COLLEGE PROGRESS[1]

THERE is an aspect of our two ancient English Universities which is apt to escape notice. We think of them as seats of learning and education, as temporary homes of athletic or studious youth, as highly organized cities of pleasure, where cricket, football, Greek, Latin, golf, and mathematics are mingled in agreeable and diverting proportions. To the artistic memory the name University suggests beautiful buildings, romantic gardens, moonlit reaches of river, the sound of bells in the night; to the frivolous memory, half mythical exploits with proctors and their myrmidons, tussles with obdurate tutors, stealthy drives in tandems, hairbreadth escapes to Ascot or to Epsom; to the studious memory, animated debating-societies, ultimate problems of Being confidently solved, long stretches of Greek and Latin text victoriously subdued. But there is one thing our colleges do not readily suggest to the mind which dwells upon academic memories; they do not suggest agriculture. And yet the college is a landlord; a steady-going, careful, impoverished landlord, vitally interested in wheat and barley and roots and artificial grasses, in pigsties and farm-buildings, and all the paraphernalia

[1] *Macmillan's Magazine*, November 1896, vol. 75. Since these words were written the carriage has given place to the motor car, the old tenures have been abolished, and the youthful outrider has become the antique Warden.

of rural life. Some of these colleges are among the oldest landlords in England, for the college is a conservative; it does not easily part with its old farms or its old tenants, or tear up its old sallow parchments and papers. Hence it is that one or two Oxford colleges farm to the present day lands which they farmed four hundred years ago, with great liberality too, as all readers of *Social England* will remember.[1] And hence, too, the student of English agriculture in the fifteenth and sixteenth centuries finds some of his most valuable material in the college muniment-rooms. Yet this bucolic side of academic life keeps modestly in the background. With the bursar indeed it is ever present, with the Fellow sometimes, with the undergraduate never. Only occasionally, should the undergraduate stay up in the vacation, will his eye catch something of this rural background to his normal existence. He will find one morning the quadrangle filled with farmers come to pay their rent, to receive the immemorial pair of white gloves at the bursary, to dine and smoke through an afternoon in the college hall. Or he will catch sight of the Warden and his attendants starting in some state from the front lodge in an open carriage, and he will learn that they are going Progress, as the phrase runs, that they are travelling upon their annual round of inspection through the college farms.

[1] There is an excellent account of the management of two New College farms, Alton Barnes and Takely, in the fifteenth century, in *Social England*, ii. 390–1. These farms are still (1896) in possession of the college.

Q

There is not, so far as we are aware, much obtainable literature about these Progresses. One document is indeed known, and has been partially printed.[1] A Fellow of Corpus Christi College in the reign of Queen Elizabeth has left a clever Latin dialogue, describing a journey taken by the President of his college and others for the purpose of holding manorial courts at Heyford and Temple Guiting. It was not a very eventful journey, nor a very romantic journey, but it was signalized by the capture of a hare, which the President appropriated—'Leporem capimus, Praeses asportavit, bellum spectaculum' (We catch a hare; the President appropriated it; a fine sight)—and by a remarkable display of levity on the part of that dignitary on the last evening at Temple Guiting, which in the interest of discipline shall be consigned to a note.[2] But we must hasten to relate our own experiences.

Once a year the Warden and Fellows of New College, Oxford, elect a young gentleman to serve as Outrider to the Warden upon his annual progress round the College estates. There is a fine open-air flavour about this term *outrider*. It suggests a blue overcoat with silver buttons and a tussle with a highwayman thrown in. It is true that all outriders are not heroes. There was a certain Mr. Outrider Squibb, who went

[1] *Dialogus de lustratione Geitonica qui inscribitur Nuttus*; Rawlinson D, 463. Passages have been printed in Doctor Fowler's *History of Corpus Christi College*.

[2] 'Mensa tollitur, Praeses chartas chartas inclamat. Lusitamus, nec oculi nostri ad duodecimam somnum vident' (the dishes are removed; the President cries for cards, cards. We play, and our eyes do not see sleep till midnight).

Progress in 1677, who would have required a different
surname to sustain the part. Nor as a matter of fact
has any outrider distinguished himself in any bold
passage of arms, so far as we are able to discover from
a hasty view of the records of the New College Progresses, which date back to 1659. But there are
weapons hung up in one of the common-rooms at
Magdalen College which imply another tale, and
speak of days when a Warden and his attendant wore
holsters at the saddle-bow, and might be trusted to
give a good account of themselves on a lonely highway
in the dim evening light. If one night, as four weary
steeds found their way across Whaddon Chase, a
pistol-shot rang into the air and swords crossed in the
moonlight, the fact has not been recorded. The thin
little note-books of the Progress, covered with a small
and crabbed writing, tell only of less exciting themes,
of fines exacted, of trees marked for felling, of copyholders admitted at the manor court, of wine and
mutton consumed at the manor farms.

The Outrider is supposed to represent the body
of Fellows upon the Progress and to keep the purse.
It would be unsafe to conjecture that he is deeply
versed in the arcana of rural life. If he can tell a
yellowhammer from a goldfinch or a hollyhock from
a larkspur he does well; he is above the average of
outriders. To identify a drill, a harrow, or an adze,
to have a fine eye for the points of a heifer, to discuss
roots and artificial grasses for five minutes without
betraying himself, to proffer an opinion on the make
of a rick or the handiwork of the village thatcher,

would be to transcend the dreams of his modest ambition. For one brief week it is permitted to him to
enjoy the subtle and gratifying sensation of being a
country landlord. In his tall silk hat and black coat
he receives with some awkwardness and some complacency the gracious welcome of his tenants, dis-
tributes doles of silver to pew-openers, schoolgirls,
and farm-servants, and marches through the village
with the proud step of a benefactor. He is part of a
corporate landlord, older than the oldest inhabitant,
older than the line of elms which rims the lane, old
as the grey church itself which peals out a pleasant
chime as the Warden's carriage swings into sight.

There was a time when these expeditions were real
voyages, for the college estates are scattered from
Wiltshire to Essex, and it used to be the custom to
visit them all yearly. A tradition still lives among
the country folk of Great Horwood in Buckinghamshire, of how one night, long ago, when the Warden
and his following were quartered in the manor farm,
a handful of malicious peasants stole into the stables
and cut off the tails of the college horses. The next
day the Progress continued towards London borne on
tailless steeds. But the Warden was a man of resource
and dignity, and somehow or other he procured a set
of false tails before the representatives of the college
reached town. It seemed that Great Horwood was
after all to be cheated of its Fescennine vengeance.
But the gods were on the side of humour, and as the
cavalcade was stepping jauntily up a crowded street,
they arranged a small but pretty catastrophe. One

of the false tails fell off, and the folk of Great Horwood chuckle over that tail to this day, and serve it up merrily with home-made cowslip wine, when July comes round again with the college gentlemen and the raspberries.

In these long pilgrimages the Progress was not inadequately sustained with creature comforts. Indeed, a stipulation used to be inserted into the college leases that the tenant should be bound to entertain the Warden and his following for a certain number of days in the year. It was no laughing affair this stipulation, for, if we may trust one record, the Progress brought with it a right Gargantuan appetite. Not for us is it to transcribe the long lists of beeves and capons and muttons with which the sons of Academe sustained their modest strength among the groves and meadows. That would need a pen steeped in Rabelaisian ink. But while we acknowledge the prowess of our predecessors with knife and fork, it is only just to ourselves to observe that what with quick trains and easy carriages the appetite now has not a fair chance to grow. If only the Warden's Progress would again take to the saddle, there might once more be Homeric dining among the college manors; and merry desolation would descend upon the farm-yard, and three black-coated gentlemen, tanned by a long day's exercise in the summer air, would perhaps once again quaff country ale by the starlit window-sill right unto the small hours of the morning.

We abbreviate these rustic rituals nowadays. It is rare for Progress to visit all the college farms in one year. This year we did not go to the Wiltshire farms, nor into Essex, nor did we pay a visit to a certain house in Gerrard Street, Soho, once famous as the residence of Edmund Burke. The Progress confined its attention to Oxfordshire and Buckinghamshire. It slipped out of Oxford by comfortable trains, slipped from comfortable trains into comfortable carriages, and returned by the same easy method to dine and sleep at home. But there are traces of an older time still discernible beneath these modern ways. When the Warden arrives at the manor farm he takes possession. The Steward will hold his court in the drawing-room or kitchen; the Warden, the Steward, and the Outrider will lunch solemnly in the dining-room with the Warden's servant to wait on them. The farmer and his wife and family will receive the Progress, will prepare the meal, deck the table with flowers, load the invaders with every delicate attention, and then, when the hour of lunch is at hand, they will suddenly vanish. The college authorities consume the cold salmon and chicken and currant tart in solitary state, only occasionally reminded by the rustle of a dress in the passage as the door opens that some country Hebe is attending to their wants.[1]

This proceeding may seem to be somewhat ungracious on our part; but it is sanctioned by custom, and the tenants are proud to conform to a practice which has so much antiquity to back it, and which lays the Progress under so heavy an obligation towards them. There is still, in fact, a certain solemnity about

[1] The custom varies with different manors.

our proceedings which we flatter ourselves is not
wholly unimpressive. The weighty manor-rolls which
are carried into the house for the Steward's use por-
tend mystery. The small knot of rustics summoned
as Homage to the manor court loiter about the door-
way with an uneasy air of importance, as if conscious
of some strange impending rite. Let us follow the
Steward into the sitting-room of the farm-house and
sit by him as he holds his court. Imagine some low
square room with brown wainscoting, hung with en-
gravings of prize cattle, and a pleasant bow-window
giving on the lawn. A chubby, red-faced peasant,
with little sleepy eyes and a shining black coat, stands
at the Steward's elbow in a high state of nervous dis-
comfort. He is the Bailiff of the Manor, who collects
the quit-rents of the copyholders and advertises the
holding of the court. Four aged rustics sit round the
wall, as far as they can get from the Steward and his
terrible big books; these are the Homage of the
Manor. Then the Bailiff pays in the quit-rents to the
Steward, and the Steward hands a paper to the Bailiff,
who reads, or rather gabbles, out its contents, leaping
wildly over commas, slaughtering syllables wholesale,
joining that which should be kept asunder, keeping
asunder that which should be joined. He is opening
the court in due form. 'Oyes, Oyes, Oyes! All
manner of persons who owe suit and service to the
Court Baron of the Warden and Scholars of Saint
Mary's College, Winchester, commonly called New
College in Oxford, now to be holden, or who have
been summoned to appear at this time and place

draw near and give your attendance, every man answering to his name.' Then the names of the Homage are called once, and the foreman is sworn in upon the Testament in the following manner. 'You, as foreman of the Homage, with the rest of your Fellows, shall inquire and true presentment make of all such things as shall be given to you in charge, and of all such other matters as shall come to your knowledge presentable at this court without fear, favour, and affection, hatred or malice to the best of your understanding. So help you God.' And after the foreman has taken the oath, the rest of the Homage follows suit, and the court applies itself to business. The word business has a hot and bustling sound, but the thing can be taken gently enough in a manor court. You may not hurry the bucolic mind. It has its times and its seasons of remembrances, and on these times and seasons Stewards of Courts Baron, like other mortals, must wait in patience. As the list of the copyholders is called over, certain names arrest the attention of the Steward, 'Why has not Sarah Jones paid her quit-rent?' The Homage replies that she has died of epilepsy. 'Whom has she left to take up the copyhold?' This is a more difficult question, for Sarah had no full-grown son. There is a period of anxious silence. At last we hear a faint murmur of 'trustees'. A member of the Homage has tentatively suggested that James Robinson, one of Sarah's trustees, should be admitted. But this, as the Steward points out, will never do. Had Sarah a son? Yes, when the Homage comes to think of it, there was a slip of a boy. 'Where

is he?' asks the Steward. That is a large question.
Sarah Jones's boy may be anywhere; there is no tell-
ing; he may be in London, or with his aunt, or with his
aunt in London. The Steward knows his men and will
not force the pace. It seems hopeless enough at the
first blush, this chase for the youthful Jones, but with
time all things may come to pass, and a speck of sunshine may settle on the Homage. So the youthful
Jones is chased gently, but persistently, from pillar
to post; from aunt to uncle, from uncle to aunt; until
the sunshine settles and the Steward is put on a fair
way towards obtaining the desired address.

Unfortunately for the lover of antiquity, a good deal
of business is now done out of court, and but for the
collection of quit-rents and an occasional admittance
and surrender, there would be little occasion for the
holding of a court at all. The solemn proclamations
made in court at the appropriate occasions by the
Bailiff of the Manor seem to postulate a larger assembly than meets the Steward nowadays. 'Oyes, Oyes,
Oyes! If any man can make any title or claim to the
copyhold tenements holden of this Manor whereof
S. died seized, let him appear and he shall be admitted,
and in default the same will be seized into the hands of
the Lord for want of a tenant. This is the first proclamation.' As the last note of this engaging invitation
dies away, the romantic spectator demands a loud
knock, an opened door, and on the threshold the vision
of a flaming rustic bandishing a pedigree in one hand
and a copy of the court-roll in another. But Romance
may propose what it will; it is something very much

the reverse of romance which disposes. The proclamation is a mere form made and entered on the books of the Manors. The Steward and the Homage know beforehand that no one will appear to be admitted; and the solemn words fall dully upon listless ears. After the third proclamation the tenement is seized into the hands of the Lord.

When the Steward has finished his inquiries he hands to the Bailiff the form for closing the court, which the Bailiff forthwith proceeds to read as follows: 'Oyes, Oyes, Oyes! All manner of persons who have appeared this day at the Court Baron of the Warden and Scholars of Saint Mary's College of Winchester in Oxford, commonly called New College in Oxford, may now depart, keeping their day and hour on a new summons. God save the Queen and the Lords of the Manor.' Then the Homage sign the proceedings, and are rewarded for their judicial toil by the present of a sovereign. And so the court dissolves, each part of it to consume its proper luncheon.

These gentle labours, sweetened with antiquity, accord well with the remaining duties of the Progress. At one village commanding a lovely view of the Chilterns, a distribution of halfpence is made among the children, and it was a pretty sight to see them grouped on the churchyard steps as the carriage drove into the village on a hot morning in July. But the main duty of the Progress is to cultivate the friendship of the farmers and their wives, and to show them that the members of the college, under whom they hold, have a real interest in their welfare. A College Progress has ceased to be a voyage of business. The quit-rents of the copyholders, which are paid in to the Steward by the Bailiffs, are but trivial sums, which might be, and often are, sent to him by post. The main revenues of the college are no longer collected on Progress. The Warden has long given over marking trees for felling; he directs no agricultural operations, orders no farm repairs; but the tenants see in him the wise and kindly landlord, who understands their lives, remembers their histories, and sympathizes with their troubles. It is a great thing for a Corporation to be able to take human shape upon an occasion, even if the incarnation should run up a bill.

There are certain villages in Oxfordshire which have stood still in a kind of happy isolation amid the maelstrom of improvement. In these villages time is regarded as of no value, and time has been unsparing of gracious influences. A clergyman told us of a farmer who had been engaged to be married twenty years, and still was in no hurry. This is the attitude appropriate to the place. In other villages civilization advances apace. The farmer's daughter goes to the High School at Oxford or Banbury, the farmer's son works for an Oxford scholarship. In many farm-houses there is a piano. Red brick and slate replace thatch and stucco, and it has become difficult in some Buckinghamshire villages to get any thatching work done. In these counties sport has become too rapid, too fashionable, too highly organized, to interest the country folk. 'In the country chase', as the admirable Daniel remarked more than eighty years ago, 'the

lithesomeness of youth is no longer excited to pursue
the animal. Attendant footmen are discontinued and
forgotten; while the active and eager rustic with a
hunting-pole, wont to be foremost, has long forsaken
the field. All the sport now consists of speed. A hare
is hurried to death by dwarf foxhounds, and a leash
murdered in a shorter period than a single one could
generally struggle for existence. The hunter boasts a
cross of blood, or in plainer phrase, a racer sufficiently
professed to render a country sweepstake doubtful.
This variation is by no means an improvement, and
can only advantage the plethoric citizen who seeks to
combat the somnolency arising from civic festivals by
a short and sudden excess of exercise.'[1]

The horses which draw the chariots of the Progress
are certainly 'not sufficiently professed to render a
country sweepstake doubtful', and we earnestly trust
that they may never attain to that pitch of excellence.
To taste the joys of the country a large measure of
indolence is clearly indispensable. A fast trotter or
flying bicycle may quicken the pulse and raise the
spirits, but they minister no food to the memory, and
time is needed to sink a landscape into the eye. That
time may be found in the ample and leisurely vehicle
which conveys the College Progress. At first we shall
not be attuned to the leisure, or be able to cultivate the
apathy, which is necessary to enjoyment. It takes
some effort to banish the discursive reason, and to
empty the mind of those preoccupations which it is
the aim of an Oxford education to encourage. But the

[1] *Rural Sports*, iv. 659.

thing can be done; and when once it is done, what can
be more delightful than this slow pilgrimage among
antique villages, thumbing, as you go, manuscript
records left by those who have gone the same rounds
more than a hundred years ago, sure of a hospitable
welcome among country folk, such as men mete out
to old friends or to their spiritual successors?

VI

THE BEAUTY OF ENGLAND[1]

THE great advantage of living in a town is the
exciting prospect of an escape into the country.
Londoners toiling at their desks day after day refresh
their thoughts with the dream of a holiday in sweet
fortifying air among the sights and scents of the
country-side, and, if they have any love for nature,
and are not the slaves of the golf-course or the tennis-
court, count the hours which divide them from this
renewal of their blood and pilgrimage of pleasure.
The more urban we become by reason of business,
the more rural we tend to be in our intimate moods.
To us the country-side brings gaiety and freedom,
immunity and repose.

It is our fashion to speak of the country as if it were
always one and the same thing, but much of the charm
of England lies in the fact that in this little island
there is not one country but many, and that our landscape is so various that it is hardly possible, except
perhaps in certain regions of the Midlands, to take a
ten-mile walk without the continual provocation of
new vistas and enchantments. In most continental
lands, and certainly in the New World, everything is
on a bigger scale, more inhuman, more monotonous,
more grandiose:

> Huge forests and unharboured heaths,
> Hills and sandy perilous wilds.

[1] Reprinted from *The Penn Country of Buckinghamshire*, 1932.

But in England the scale of the scenery is part of its subtle attraction. Even our great views, as the prospect of the Saxon Weald seen from Hindhead, or the flats of Worcestershire as they appear to the spectator from the crown of the Malverns, or the lush green pasture-land which unrolls itself beneath the western front of the Chilterns, disclose an almost infinite variety and hold out a promise to the walker, as he descends into the plain, of a long series of thrills and excitements.

That our moist climate, which spoils so many a summer entertainment, contributes much to the gentle and delicate harmonies of the English scene will perhaps be most evident to those who have passed part of their lives in countries where the sun beats down fiercely on the land, turning pastures to a dull russet, and deep brawling rivers into dry, pebbly, inhospitable channels. Our English landscape painters, led by J. M. W. Turner, have been quick to see what can be made of a soft water-laden atmosphere, and with what ethereal gossamer effects the artist may invest his canvas by attending to the shifting lights and shades of our dappled skies. Indeed, an eminent French observer conjectures that it is this atmosphere of mist and cloud and subtle half-lights which has made our great school of English landscape painters. Certainly the sense of these delicate light effects has been educated to a fine point of perfection with us. Canaletto's English landscapes, beautiful as they are, show that even that sensitive Italian painter never entirely caught the ethereal glamour of England, but could not help seeing us under the sharper and harder colours of his native sky.

The intermixture of woodland and ploughland, of pasture and heath, of hill and vale, of close-shaven down and little villages nestling among the elms— all bathed in the soft light with which we are familiar, strikes the foreign visitor to England as something distinctive and peculiar to ourselves. Even our fields are, by reason of their fine hedgerows and hedgerow elms, distinguished from the dead and disconsolate flats of Northern France and Germany, and are so well timbered that on a distant view, a fertile English plain appears in summer to be covered with forest foliage. This dispersion of noble timber, which we may trace to its historical origin in the enclosures of the sixteenth century, is not to be found in a land of peasant holders, and gives to our farms an air of careless, uneconomic aristocracy.

And how beautiful are our English woods! I am not thinking of the new plantations of Douglas firs, which the science of modern forestry is spreading through the country, but of the splendid old woods of England, such as the beechwoods of the Chilterns or Burley Wood in the New Forest or the oaks of Selwood, none of which is so vast as to be unfriendly, but offers to the senses of the wayfarer as he saunters beneath its leafy aisles the clear notes and flashing wings of its engaging inhabitants, the birds. The oak, the beech, the elm, and, to a lesser degree, the ash are *par excellence* English trees; but our older woods are apt also to be enriched by the dark green of the holly, which, under a winter sky, when the high stems are stripped of their leaves, gives a depth of vivid colouring to the scene.

The streams and rivers of England partake of the same general character of friendliness, flowing flush with their banks and not so swiftly but that a canoe can, almost anywhere, be paddled upstream. Even in a long summer drought England is full of flowing water, and that farmer is singular in his misfortune who can find no ready means of giving his cattle to drink.

In a country so generous and hospitable to man the signs of ancient settlements are almost everywhere visible. The earliest English atlas—that of Saxton, of which I possess a beautiful copy from the library of my old friend Mr. Yates Thompson—shows how thickly settled was our country-side in the reign of Queen Elizabeth. Our smallest villages have pedigrees which put the oldest families to shame. So ancient are many of our rustic settlements that they seem to have grown into the landscape, and to have become an indistinguishable part of surrounding nature. Indeed, it is difficult to conjure up the image of English country without thinking at the same time of our old villages and of the cottage gardens with their

> gold-dusted snapdragon,
> Sweet William with its homely cottage smell,
> And stocks in fragrant blow

which glow above the powdery country roads under the midsummer sky.

The unique and incommunicable beauty of the English landscape constitutes for most Englishmen the strongest of all the ties which bind them to their country. However far they travel, they carry the English landscape in their hearts. As the scroll of memory unwinds itself, scene after scene returns with its complex association of sight and hearing, the emerald green of an English May, the carpet of primroses in the clearing, the pellucid trout-stream, the fat kine browsing in the park, the cricket matches on the village green, the church spire pointing upwards to the pale-blue sky, the fragrant smell of wood fires, the butterflies on chalk hills, the lark rising from the plough into the March wind, or the morning salutation of blackbird or thrush from the garden laurels. These and many other notes blend in a harmony the elements of which we do not attempt to disentangle, for each part communicates its sweetness to the other.

We cannot afford to have these associations disturbed by the intrusion of alien and vulgar things. It will be very easy to spoil our English scenery. Much of what is most beautiful is already ruined, for it is as delicate as the English wild rose and flutters to pieces at a touch! But with a little goodwill and resolution we may still preserve the beauties which remain.

VII

THE REAL OXFORD MOVEMENT[1]

'DR. WINCHESTER', wrote Edward Gibbon of his former tutor at Magdalen, 'well remembered that he had a salary to receive, and only forgot that he had a duty to perform.' The torpor of Oxford in the eighteenth century, the Oxford of Gibbon, of Adam Smith, and of Bentham, has become proverbial and serves as a foil, in the popular imagination, to the general enlivenment of the University in the succeeding age. It is presumably for this reason that a certain religious and theological excitement which caught Oxford in the early years of Queen Victoria's reign is commonly described and accepted as The Oxford Movement. It is not my purpose to dwell upon that 'true and noble effort', that 'short scene of religious earnestness and aspiration with all that was in it of self-devotion, affectionateness, and high and refined and varied character', which has been described with so much feeling and eloquence by Dean Church, its historian. If it is alluded to here, it is only that we may remind ourselves that there have been other Oxford movements before and since, movements not less noble, in their original intention, not less far-reaching in their ultimate effect, a Scholastic movement, a Lollard movement, a Methodist movement, a move-

---

[1] Being part of the Rhys Roberts Lecture delivered before the Royal College of Physicians on November 14, 1929. Reprinted from *The Contemporary Review*.

ment for the improvement of artistic taste, for the establishment of settlements of University men in the slums of our great towns, and again for the spread of extra-mural instruction among adults. There is, in fact, no one Oxford Movement. England, writes Emerson, 'is the land of mixture and surprise; and when you have settled it that the universities are moribund, out comes a poetic influence from the heart of Oxford to mould the opinions of cities, to build their houses as simply as birds their nests, to give veracity to art and cleanse mankind, as an appeal to moral order always must'.

The movement of which I wish to speak here belongs to the secular and not to the ecclesiastical sphere. For ten important years, from 1649 to 1659, Oxford was the centre of those active and distinguished discussions and investigations which afterwards fructified in the establishment of the Royal Society. It was here that Dr. Wilkins, the Warden of Wadham, with Seth Ward, Ralph Bathurst, Dr. Petty, Dr. Willis, and others held every week 'an experimental philosophical club', meeting first at Dr. Petty's, 'in an apothecary's house for the convenience of inspecting drugs', and then at the lodgings of the Warden of Wadham. It was in Oxford that these early meetings were held, from Oxford that some of the most distinguished of the original members of the group were drawn. It was an Oxford man, Thomas Sprat, afterwards Bishop of Rochester, who four years after its foundation traced the early history of the Society with an enthusiasm which has not lost its charm and freshness with the lapse of two centuries and a half.

It would be doing Oxford too much honour to trace this sudden and brilliant flowering of scientific curiosity to any fundamental revolution in the academic curriculum, or enduring triumph of the rational spirit. We are still far from the days of complete academic toleration. The Oxford which was the nursery of the Royal Society not so very long afterwards publicly burned Hobbes's *Leviathan* and acquiesced in the expulsion of John Locke from his Studentship at Christ Church. But during the Civil Wars and throughout the uneasy period of the Protectorate there was developed a tendency, which was evidenced also more recently during the Great War, to embark upon new studies and to break the crust of intellectual habit. Sick of theological dissensions and despairing of public affairs, students turned to Nature and to those methods of eliciting Nature's secrets which had been recommended by the genius of Francis Bacon. The original and natural centre for the prosecution of such studies was, of course, not Oxford, but the capital of the country. London had the Royal College of Physicians, and to the physician there was nothing new in a science of observation and experiment created to serve a practical purpose. Accordingly, about the year 1646, a small scientific club consisting mainly of doctors, but containing also some earnest inquirers who were not of the profession, was formed for the discussion of scientific problems of every description, and met weekly in the rooms of Dr. Jonathan Goddard, afterwards Warden of Merton.

The 'invisible college', as it was called, had but a short life. Partly by reason of personal accidents, and partly because the political and religious atmosphere of London became uncomfortable to students of moderate or cavalier views, the chief activities of the movement were transferred to the groves and courts of Oxford. Here was comparative leisure, here was an atmosphere not indeed wholly, but to a large extent, free from religious fanaticism, and here was an intellectual society which had for some years past been quickened by the breath of the new curiosity. 'The University', writes Sprat, 'had at that time many members of its own who had begun a free way of reasoning; and was also frequented by some gentlemen of Philosophical Minds whom the misfortunes of the kingdom and the security and ease of a retirement among town men had drawn thither.' Among its own members were Wilkins of Wadham, Bathurst of Trinity, and two young men of outstanding genius, Christopher Wren of Wadham and Robert Hooke of Christ Church; among strangers drawn to Oxford for one reason or another were Robert Boyle and William Petty, the founder of English statistical science. Two distinguished Cambridge mathematicians, John Wallis and Seth Ward, holding respectively the newly founded Savilian Chairs for Mathematics and Astronomy, were of the same circle.

In every wide intellectual movement there are men who exercise an influence quite out of relation to the importance of their positive contribution to the advancement of knowledge. Of such was John Wilkins, Warden of Wadham from 1648 to 1659. He was not prolific as a writer, for his publications— spread over a long life—are contained in two octavo volumes. Nor is his name associated with any great scientific discovery, but he stimulated others by the glow of his active and comprehensive curiosity and made the tenure of his Oxford office memorable in the history of English science by gathering together the men and presiding over the discussions out of which the Royal Society ultimately took shape.

Wilkins, 'that most obliging and universally curious Dr. Wilkins', as Evelyn dubbed him, though destined for a bishopric, was primarily a man of science whose vigorous mind had been excited by the new Copernican astronomy and by the writings of Kepler, Galileo, and Bacon. To popularize the new philosophy and to defend it against the strong countervailing force of theological opinion was his first concern. His early writings were directed to prove that there may be another habitable world in the moon, with which it might be possible to communicate, and that the earth itself was one of the planets. His interests, however, were not confined to astronomical physics. The son of an Oxford goldsmith, he had clever hands as well as mechanical instincts, and an ingenious forward-reaching mind. He contrived a speaking statue and apiaries of glass. Holding that 'our last and most divine knowledge is intended for action', he wrote a treatise entitled

Mathematical Magic, to illustrate the operation of the balance, the lever, the wheel, the pulley, the wedge, and the screw, embarking in a field of study which he describes as 'one of the most easy, pleasant, useful, and yet most neglected parts of mathematics not before treated of in this language'. He had schemes for a sailing chariot, a submarine boat, and a flying machine; but what was more important than any one of his personal schemes or experiments was his sense of the need of scientific collaboration, his excellence in communication, and his rare faculty, based upon good nature, sympathy, and abounding animal vigour, of attaching to himself the men who were then doing important work in any line of scientific inquiry.[1] It was a letter from Wilkins which in 1654 induced Robert Boyle to cross the Channel and to settle in Oxford. That rare genius, 'a corpuscularian without Epicurus, a great and happy analyser addicted to no particular sect, but as becomes a generous and free philosopher preferring truth above all',[2] lived in Oxford for fourteen years, and the visitor who gazes upon the low dome of the Shelley Memorial in the High Street may reflect that it was on this spot, or not far from it, that Boyle carried out the experiments which have made his name immortal, here that he wrote his three classical treatises, the *New Experiments Concerning the Spring of the Air, the Sceptical*

---

[1] *The Life and Times of John Wilkins*, by P. A. Wright Henderson.

[2] *Evelyn's Diary and Correspondence*, ed. Wheatley, iii. 479–89.

Chymist, and the *Experiments and Considerations touching Colour*, and here that, with the assistance of Hooke, he invented the air-pump which is the parent of the steam-engine and so the distant source of modern industrial civilization.

An equally remarkable visitor adopted into the College society of Oxford at that time was William Petty, by turns a cabin-boy, a hawker, and a seaman, who, returning to England in 1646 after a course of medical studies abroad, was made first a Fellow and then Vice-Principal of Brasenose. Petty was one of those energetic, original, quick-thinking men who make a stir wherever they go. Not content with imparting novelty and reality to his anatomical lectures by the introduction of a corpse, he startled the country by reviving a young woman named Ann Green who, having been hanged for murder, was presented to the doctors for dissection. But it was a common characteristic of this brilliant Oxford group that they were not content with a narrow specialism. Petty was only incidentally a physician. His *Observations on the London Bills of Mortality*, published under the name of his friend and helper, Captain Graunt, in 1662, and his *Essays on Political Arithmetic*, rank among the classics of our economic literature. He was the first Englishman who brought into the study of political problems the notions of number, quantity, measurement, ˋthe first to attempt a scientific estimate of national wealth, the first to seize the economic importance of man-power. His miscellaneous papers, a selection of which has recently been admirably edited by his descendant, Lord Lansdowne, show the span and practical nature of his activities. Now he designs a double-keel boat, now frames a scheme for land registration or advocates a Council of Trade and the adoption of a definite policy for the political and social future of England and Ireland. He was sometimes, in the exercise of his favourite pastime of 'ratiocination', a little fantastic, but always independent of tradition and authority, and often, as when he advocated the study of comparative anatomy and occupational diseases, in advance of his time. Few thinkers in the seventeenth century have foreshadowed in their writings so many improvements of a later age.

Petty was one of the Wadham group, and an original member of the Royal Society; but he was only for two years a resident in Oxford. A great part of his life was spent in Ireland, where he carried out with infinite skill and patience, and amid a storm of obloquy and detraction which would have quailed any spirit less stout than his, the land survey on which was based the Cromwellian Settlement. It was characteristic of his practical sagacity that in the process of executing the 'Down' survey he made a fortune for himself, and equally characteristic that wealth was no invitation to indolence. 'The man', said Charles II, 'will not be content to be excellent, but is still aiming at impossible things.' Discovery and contention were his master passions. At the St. Andrew's Day dinner of the Royal Society in 1687 he fell into a dispute with another member as to the weight of woods, arguing that of all woods quince was the heaviest, and this

with so much passion that, having grown very gouty
and corpulent, he went home ill, and a few days afterwards died.

In the brilliant company which met weekly to
exhibit and discuss scientific experiments and ideas
at Wadham—a college where even the manciple was
a skilled maker of mathematical instruments with
apparently no injurious results upon the cuisine—
there was a lad of miraculous precocity, who, unlike
most precocious children, continued to grow in intellectual stature, and made for himself in a few short
years the best kind of national reputation. Christopher Wren came up to Wadham as a Fellow Commoner in 1646. He was then only fourteen years of
age, but already an ingenious inventor, a brilliant
geometrician, and an accomplished Latinist. Everything which he touched turned to gold. Nothing was
too big for him and nothing too small. If he had not
lived to be the greatest architect of his age he would
have been in all probability the first of its geometri-
cians, astronomers, or anatomists. The charm and
simplicity of his nature, the prodigality of his inventive
powers, the singular union in him of artistic taste
with the gifts of the exact scientific thinker and the
shrewd instinct of the practical man, disarmed all
opposition and conquered from the first the admiration of those who knew him. In the *Parentalia*, or
Family Memoirs, published by his grandson, there
is a list of the 'new theories, inventions, experiments,
and mechanical improvements exhibited by Mr. Wren
at the first assemblies in Wadham College'. The list

contains fifty-three items and deals with every kind of subject, the moon's libration, engraving, whale-fishing, music, architecture, carriage-building, ribbon-making, marine observation, anatomy, mining, upon all of which and many other themes the dancing fancy of this very young gentleman was intelligently and curiously playing.

At the age of twenty-five Wren was made Professor of Astronomy at Gresham College, which became the first home of the Royal Society. His inaugural address was all that a lecture should be: learned, imaginative, full of sanguine anticipations for the progress of his science; but though he helped to make improvements in the telescope, as in the barometer, and was the first to essay a measured selenography, the subject of his chair never held his exclusive attention. He discovered mezzotint, made experiments in the transfusion of blood, and interested himself in projects for the measurement and recording of meteorological phenomena. More and more, however, he was drawn towards architecture by his native taste, his geometrical sense and his rare powers of delicate and exact drafts-manship. The Fire of London gave him his opportunity—London, 'the great city which it is pity in the opinion of her neighbours should longer continue the most unadorned of her bigness in the world'; and hardly had the ashes cooled before he sent in to the King a plan for its reconstruction.

The great national tasks on which Wren was henceforth engaged did not snap his connexion with Oxford, to which University he was pleasurably bound by a

Fellowship at All Souls and from 1660 onwards by the Savilian Chair of Astronomy. His successive plans for St. Paul's Cathedral are among the principal treasures of the Codrington Library. But it is not only here that we must look for the continuing signs of his presence in Oxford. The Sheldonian Theatre, the Old Ashmolean Museum,[1] and the majestic front of Christ Church, attest his handiwork and constitute the noblest of all the memorials which a son of Oxford has bequeathed to the nursing mother of his mind.

In the year 1654, when Dr. Wilkins and his young men were in full blast, the University received a visit from John Evelyn, who supped at a magnificent entertainment at Wadham on the invitation of his dear and excellent friend the Warden. Fourteen years before, Evelyn, the son of a Surrey squire and reared among the poetic groves of Wotton, had been a Fellow Commoner of Balliol, and though he had profited little from the academic studies which then prevailed in Oxford, he loved his old University and was determined to serve it. Returning to Oxford after a long spell of travel, during which he had made a study of the scientific and artistic collections of France and Italy, Evelyn was struck by the contrast between the speculative energy of the Wadham group and the poverty of the material equipment provided by the University. The mathematical instruments at St. John's were for the most part the gift of Archbishop Laud. The Physics Garden contained no extraordinary curiosities, the Anatomy School nothing

[1] Gunther, *Early Science in Oxford*, iii. 293–5.

extraordinary 'save the skin of a jackal, a rarely
coloured jacatoo or prodigious large parrot, and two
humming-birds not much bigger than one bumble-
bee'. But in the lodgings and gallery at Wadham
there was 'a variety of shadows, dyals, perspectives,
and many other artificial, mathematical, and magical
curiosities, a way wiser and thermometer, a monstrous
magnet, conic and other sections, a ballance or demi-
circle, most of the Warden's own devising'. Moreover, there was that 'prodigious young scholar Mr.
Christopher Wren'.

The associations which Evelyn then made with the
Oxford scientific movement were continued through
the remainder of his life. An original member of the
Royal Society and an enthusiastic believer in its work,
Evelyn was concerned to argue that the Universities
should regard the Society as 'a colony of their own
planting' and in no sense as a countervailing or rival
influence. His own loyalty was impartially distributed.
If he obtained the Arundel Library for the Society,
he was the means of securing the Arundel marbles
for Oxford. In common with many other members
of the Oxford group Evelyn harnessed much of his
intellectual energy to the service of the State. His
great work on forest trees was undertaken at the
request of the Commissioners of the Navy, who were
concerned by the waste and destruction of our English
woods during the Civil Wars and apprehensive of the
growing dependence of English marine power on sea-
borne supplies. Evelyn's *Silva* was widely read and
deservedly admired, and, if it be true, as he alleges,

that 'many million timber trees' were planted 'by the direction of this work',[1] there may be some justification for Isaac Disraeli's statement that the ships of Nelson were made possible by the science and forethought of John Evelyn.

Like the Petty papers, the letters and diaries of Evelyn are full of those forward-reaching notions which are the note of the whole movement. The modern reformers who advocate a system of simplified spelling and the introduction of new accents to mark pronunciation will find that the accomplished Surrey virtuoso has been before them.[2] It is to his credit also that he proposed that collections should be made of country dialects and proverbs as well as of the technical, exotic, and pure English words in the language, that he wrote a treatise for the abatement of London smoke, and was the first to advocate a more careful printing of school books. But for Cowley's death and the Plague of London he might have been successful in creating an organization which would have anticipated alike the British Academy and the Oxford Dictionary of the English language.

A year after the visit to Oxford which introduced Evelyn to that 'prodigious young genius Mr. Wren', the Oxford group of scientific thinkers were reinforced by the addition of a young servitor from Christ Church who, like Wren, was destined to make himself illustrious as a man of science and an architect. In temperament and physique no two men could be more

---

[1] *Diaries*, ed. Wheatley, iii. 463.
[2] See *Diaries*, iii. 309, and iv. 3 ff.

different than Christopher Wren and Robert Hooke. Wren possessed every physical endowment which Nature can bestow. His face was alive with a sensitive and captivating beauty; he was healthy and well-bred, brimful of animal spirits and geniality towards men. Hooke, with a brain not less acute and an intellectual curiosity not less comprehensive, suffered from the evils of a wretched physique and a melancholy, mistrustful, and jealous temper. Wren went through life adding to his friends. Hooke was one of those unhappy men of genius who, out of jealousy and overwork, multiply the personal jars of life and get themselves involved in harassing lawsuits. Yet the two men had much in common. Each was a mechanical genius. Each was accomplished in physical speculations. Each was an architect. Each sent in a plan for the rebuilding of London after the Fire. While Wren designed St. Paul's, Hooke was the architect of the Royal College of Physicians in Warwick Lane, of Bedlam, and of Montague House, which is now the British Museum.

It is a note of young men of genius to scatter their powers over a wide field. Hooke shared with Wren that intoxication of universal curiosity which was common in those golden years of Oxford fellowship in scientific pursuits. He helped Boyle with his air-pump, popularized the microscope, discovered the cellular structure of plants, improved the pendulum under Seth Ward's directions, and presented Wilkins with more than thirty designs for a flying machine which he had devised while yet a schoolboy at Westminster. Where, however, Hooke differed from Wren was that, while Wren learnt to concentrate upon the line of his highest powers, Hooke never outlived the prodigality of his youthful inventiveness. His is the singular case of a man who might have been more famous had his mind been less active. With rare powers of reasoning and divination, with astonishing fertility of scientific resource, and a firm grasp of scientific method, he just missed supreme greatness for lack of concentration. Perhaps we may attribute this to physical weakness, perhaps to a certain flaw in character, perhaps to the nature of his office of Curator to the Royal Society, which bound him to make provision for the exhibition of three or four experiments at each weekly meeting, a prodigious draft upon the energies of a delicate man. Thus, while he had the capacity to divine the law of gravitation, it was left to Newton to prove it. So it was with many of Hooke's discoveries. He illumined wide territories for others to annex and make their own.

It may be asked how far the many-sided outburst of intellectual energy which is thus briefly described left a permanent mark on the studies of Oxford. In the history of the great human movements of head and heart, the main work of fertilizing irrigation is often carried on in regions far remote from the fountain-head. So it has been more than once with Oxford. So it was with Lollardry, the flame which burnt brightly in many a charcoal-burner's hovel among the beech-woods of the Chilterns long after it had been stifled by persecution in the Oxford colleges. So also was it with

Methodism. What, however, are we to think of the passionate impulse of scientific curiosity which during ten years in the middle of the seventeenth century took possession of the soul of Oxford? Is it possible that a movement associated with such famous names and full of so momentous a future should have passed through Oxford without effecting a transformation in the whole intellectual outlook of the place? The answer is, we believe, not that the Wadham movement failed to exercise a continuing influence in moulding a rational habit of mind, but that this influence was disappointingly small in relation to the possibilities. Why was this? Oxford was royalist and the King was notoriously favourable to the Royal Society and all its works. Oxford was orthodox, but so were her scientific leaders, who were carefully insured with the Anglican Church. Yet the atmosphere of the place from the Restoration onwards seems in many ways to have been subtly unfavourable to a great extension of the scientific domain.

Men of science still lived and worked in the University, but without exercising any general influence on its intellectual life. There can, indeed, be no more significant illustration of the way in which Oxford, having for a decade held the lead in co-operative scientific inquiry, suddenly lost it, than the fact that John Mayow, who entered Wadham as a Commoner in 1658 and afterwards proceeded to All Souls, an original chemist, worthy in the opinion of many good judges to rank with Boyle, carried on his researches at All Souls, discovering oxygen and grasping the essential secrets about the formation of oxides and acids in such isolation that Newton, and even Boyle, seem to have been unaware of his published work.[1] Only by slow and painful degrees, and not till many an academic battle had been fought, did science recover that position of eminence in our most ancient University which had belonged to it through personal and political accidents when Christopher Wren was a youth and in the fresh glory of his transcendent powers, and when every generous mind was eagerly turning from the disastrous and sterile battle of the creeds to the new and peaceful pastures of natural knowledge.

[1] Gunther, *Early Science in Oxford*, i. 31 ff.

VIII

GLADSTONE AND IRELAND[1]

IN the disastrous eclipse of liberty now darkening the continent of Europe the name of Gladstone recovers something of its original lustre. Scholars and publicists, not in Britain only, are drawn to the great Liberal and Christian humanist, whose faith in moral forces and in the healing virtues of freedom marks him out so distinctly from the sinister figures who dominate the European scene. Morley's three-volume biography, full and substantial as it is, no longer suffices. New monographs proceed in showers from the Press. New biographies, notably those of Chamberlain and Carnarvon, shed fresh light on passages where uncertainty previously prevailed, and now comes that distinguished historian and publicist, Dr. Hammond, in whom the Liberal faith is as ardent as ever, with a full, satisfying and eloquent treatise on the most important of all Gladstone's political dealings, his relations with Ireland.

As was only to be expected, Dr. Hammond has a deep veneration for Gladstone's great qualities, for his European sense, his steady moral and religious fervour, his prodigious capacity for work, his high standard of public duty, and noble gift of speech. He has no difficulty, from the ample stores of knowledge which now lie to his hand, in demonstrating the fallacy of

[1] *Gladstone and the Irish Nation*, by J. L. Hammond. Reprinted from *The Spectator*, Nov. 4, 1938. (Longmans, Green. 36s.)

the most grievous charges to which in the heat of a bitter party conflict Gladstone was exposed; such as that he had adopted a policy of Home Rule for Ireland in the autumn and winter of 1885 from a desire for office, or that a taint of dishonour and hypocrisy rests on his dealings with Parnell. Gladstone is for him 'the loyal Minister of the Queen, the faithful servant of the nation, the glory of the Parliament'.

But, at the same time, he notes certain blemishes which, though not detracting from Gladstone's stature as a man, make him less effective as a Prime Minister than he might have been. His tact in dealing with individuals was by no means equal to his skill in the managing of assemblies. He was singularly unfortunate, for instance, in his handling of Chamberlain and Hartington. His power of intense concentration on the subject in hand prevented him from using a balanced judgement over a wide field of politics. Thus, while justice to Ireland had been present to his mind as an urgent problem as far back as 1845, it was long displaced by a succession of other interests further removed from the centre of British politics; by Italy and Bulgaria, by Afghanistan and Egypt, by the Zulus and the Boers. Indeed it was not till the latest stage of his long career that Gladstone regarded himself as having a mission to bring justice to Ireland. In his Second Administration, when he felt himself compelled by force of circumstances to pass the Land Act of 1881, 'the most revolutionary measure that passed through Parliament in the nineteenth century', he was so far from regarding himself as harnessed to the Irish

question that he contemplated an exchange of the
active for the contemplative life. Homer and Dante,
Augustine and Butler, and all the splendid resources
of the Hawarden library were tugging at his heart. His
view was that he had retired from active politics in
1874, and that he was only brought back by the Bulgarian atrocities.

Thus there was a curious spirit of improvisation
and attendance on events in his treatment of the Irish
question. The Land Act of 1881 was launched upon
the world without any previous inquiry by a Royal
Commission into the Irish land question. No Irish
leaders were taken into consultation. The main part
of the Bill was drafted single-handed by the Prime
Minister himself. Finally, while the Prime Minister
at the age of thirty-six had been impressed by Guizot
with the importance of bringing justice to Ireland, he
only once visited the island (1877) and then without
seeing any of the things which a statesman having
Irish interests at heart should have been at pains to
notice. In view of the importance of keeping touch
with the leaders of Irish opinion, it was a major
tragedy that Gladstone established so little direct
contact with Parnell. But Parnell was guilty of an
offence which in the eyes of a great English Parliamentarian was unforgivable. He defied the British
Parliament and deliberately tried to make it ridiculous
and unworkable. Any other sin would have been by
comparison venial. For Gladstone, steeped in reverence for Parliament, for its tradition, its dignity,
its forms, its great services to the cause of human

freedom, this sin was mortal and a fatal blow to friendly intercourse.

The intellectual influences which moulded Gladstone's mind were other than those which might have been expected to fashion the thoughts of a great English Liberal parliamentarian. Unlike Salisbury, he was foreign to the new scientific knowledge of his age. The seminal minds in the English Liberal movement, Locke, Bentham, Adam Smith, meant little to him. As Dr. Hammond points out, his spiritual roots were in religion and poetry, in the Bible and Homer, in Dante and Butler, and so from men like Chamberlain, who were little versed in the great tradition of European humanism, he felt a sense of estrangement. It is curious to note, too, how faintly his mind was touched with the need for developing the social services. When Chamberlain, with his splendid record of municipal improvements in Birmingham, was first invited into the Cabinet, he was offered, with a curious lack of discernment, the Admiralty, and when this had been declined, and the Irish or Colonial Offices, fields in which his great administrative talents might have been brilliantly deployed, had also been denied to him, was finally fobbed off with the Local Government Board, and there starved of effective legislative opportunity.

Dr. Hammond makes a good point when he observes that it was a misfortune that Gladstone spent so much time at the Treasury, for though his strict sense of financial responsibility was most valuable to the country, spreading its influence through local administration, it had also its unfortunate side. England and Ireland both wanted a great deal more public money spent upon them. Gladstone grudged every penny:

'He was really a man in whom a luminous European sense struggled with the spirit of a high-principled miser, a great catholic genius with a pedantic reverence for the precedents and traditions of Whitehall. He was a high-principled miser because he firmly believed, as the best men among whom he had spent his youth believed, that the misery of the poor was due chiefly to the public extravagance, and the waste and misuse of the nation's finances. Send his imagination over the mountains of Europe and he had the eye of an eagle. Shut him up in the Treasury cupboards and he was like a captured hawk whose eyes have been sealed.'

And yet what extraordinary qualities were shown in Gladstone's long campaign for the redress of Irish grievances! What persistence under disappointments and misfortunes! What inexhaustible courage and resource! What faith, magnanimity, and insight in refusing to be deterred by Irish crime and Irish calumny from pressing forward with his plans for the righting of Irish wrongs! The Queen wrecked his plan for the establishment of a Court in Ireland. The Bishops foiled his design for an Irish University. The Parliaments, which were called upon to consider his remedial proposals, debated in an atmosphere of agrarian crime and Irish hostility. At one relatively hopeful moment came the Phoenix Park murders, at another, just when Parnell had been cleared of the charges brought against him by *The Times* newspaper and it seemed at last as if the Home Rule ship were coming into harbour, came the shattering news of the Irish leader's undefended divorce suit, and the ruinous split in the Irish Party. Yet despite this malignant turn of events, with almost all the British intellectuals arrayed against him, with a most slender supporting majority and a formidable front Opposition bench waiting to trip him up in the House of Commons and certain defeat impending in the Lords, Gladstone at the age of eighty-four passed his final, long, and intricate Home Rule Bill through the House. Never has there been so great, so astonishing a parliamentary performance.

Dr. Hammond will have the assent of many good judges in regarding the defeat of this measure as a signal misfortune. Had it been passed the Renaissance of Irish culture might, as he suggests, have been associated with a friendly spirit towards England, and have been as cordial as it is now suspicious and remote. We might have been spared the miserable episode of the gunmen. Our public men might have known more of one another, for the Ireland of to-day, save for the six Northern counties, is in the hands of men who have less knowledge of Englishmen than the leaders of the old Irish Parliamentary Party. Yet would Ulster, even in those days, have loyally accepted a Dublin Parliament? Bryce, an Ulster man, with some rebel blood in his veins, had doubts. But if Gladstone may be criticized, as Bryce criticized him, for having insufficiently weighed the claims of Ulster, it was because he believed that only a single Parliament for

all Ireland could satisfy the imagination of the Irish
nation.

The hatred against Gladstone in his own lifetime
was terrific, the detraction unceasing. His deep religious convictions and his essential conservatism did
not save him from the scorn and animosity of the
well-born and the wealthy. Yet he was the greatest
popular leader of his age, and this because he offered
to the working classes, 'not material bribes' but, as
Dr. Hammond rightly observes, 'something to satisfy
their self-respect'. It is altogether to the credit of
British democracy that so many of the poor and dis-
inherited responded to that appeal.

Among the Irish characters depicted by Dr. Hammond in this long and brilliant volume one only is
wholly attractive. Michael Davitt, the Fenian and
ex-convict who founded the Land League, is one of
the saints of Irish nationalism. This poor peasant lad
from Mayo, who at the age of eleven had lost an arm
as a cotton operative in a Lancashire factory, was later
sentenced to a term of fifteen years' imprisonment
for collecting arms and released on ticket of leave in
1877 when he had nearly served half his term. What
he suffered in his successive prisons is a grim commentary on the penal methods which then prevailed:

'During the ten months he spent at Millbank he was allowed
in all twenty minutes' conversation. During the whole time
he was at Dartmoor he was never allowed to receive a visitor.
. . . On one occasion he was handcuffed to a man out of his
mind when travelling by train.'

Yet these severities, terrible as they were, did not alter

the large scope and generosity of Davitt's nature. Parnell, the Protestant landowner of Anglo-American origin, was a proud, bitter, resentful man. Davitt, though a member of the party of violence, was not resentful, but inspired by a passionate love of Ireland and a desire to bring more happiness into the lives of the poor throughout the world. Dr. Hammond proceeds to note that in him Arnold Toynbee found a congenial spirit, and from this speculates upon the loss which Ireland suffered through the death of Arnold Toynbee in 1883, following that of T. H. Green in March 1882. The teaching of these two great Oxford men was an important humanizing influence in political thought. Yet their message had surely been delivered, and through the lips of their zealous disciples was fast permeating an ever-widening circle, before Gladstone had assailed the sanctity of contract in his Land Act or was fully embarked on the later stages of his Irish campaign.

IX

JOHN MORLEY[1]

b. 1838

IT was a shock to learn that a century had passed since the birth of John Morley,[1] whose friendship I had the privilege of enjoying for some twenty-five years, and yet as I reflect upon the present scene and compare it with the world into which Morley was born, with the principles which he preached, the causes for which he strove, and the hopes which he entertained, I reconcile myself to the thought of that long flight of years, and of Morley as a receding hero of the Victorian past.

The disciple of J. S. Mill and Comte, the friend of Meredith, Frederic Harrison, of Cotter Morison and Leslie Stephen, of Mazzini and Clemenceau; the close associate in his early radical activities of Joseph Chamberlain; the lieutenant in the Cabinets of Gladstone, Campbell-Bannerman, and Asquith, he belonged to the Augustan age of British Liberalism, living to witness many triumphs for freedom, but ultimately in the War and its train of ensuing evils experiencing a shattering defeat for the hopes of a lifetime.

In what order of gravity he would have ranked the calamities of the present age—the paralysis of international trade, the fanatical convulsions of Russia,

[1] A speech delivered at the Morley Centenary Luncheon given by the Cobden Club. Reprinted from *John O'London's Weekly*, vol. xl, no. 1027.

the resurgent militarism of the Germans, the eclipse of Italian freedom—I cannot say. But we may assume that the case of Italy would have touched him in a peculiarly tender spot, for among the literary projects of his later life was a biography of Cavour, that Italian friend of Cobden who alone among continental statesmen successfully transplanted English Liberalism into a foreign land, and whose emancipating work is now in the third generation of the Italian kingdom emphatically renounced and overthrown.

Though it is altogether right and proper that the Cobden Club should celebrate John Morley—for he was a staunch free-trader to the end, and author of the standard biography of Richard Cobden—economics were always for him, as for other original members of the Club such as James Bryce and George Otto Trevelyan, a subordinate interest. For the refinements of economic speculation he had as little taste or aptitude as for metaphysics and theology. He inhaled free-trade with his native Lancashire air, held it to be the unassailable foundation of British commercial prosperity, the safest warrant for a widespread Empire, the surest guarantee against political corruption, the strongest of many ways in which the nations of the world might be helped against the ruinous folly of war.

Primarily he was a man of letters, who, beginning as a penniless free-lance journalist, ultimately by force of brain and character as by an inner grace of nature won a position of wide intellectual influence throughout the country. This he did though devoid of many popular arts which bring renown to a journalist. His style lacked ease and fluency. He had no eye for news, no sympathy with the trivialities most likely to arrest the idle attention of the shallow multitude. The qualities which in Mill's words went to make him 'the most valuable kind of writer for the general public' were of a different order. A determination to mould opinion rather than to follow it, an active, challenging, searching mind, indignantly contemptuous of complacency and convention, a passion for the splendours of literature, a grave and constant concern with large problems of social and intellectual interest, and with all this a prose style which, while sometimes cumbrous and complex and failing of the mark through excess of ambition, is always, even in casual letters and on postcards, strong and vital, and often distinguished by passages of rare beauty and eloquence.

His special excellence lay in the field of historical biography. Here in his five English and three French biographies he opened out before his fellow countrymen a wide panorama of helpful and for the most part unfamiliar knowledge, which was all the more effective since it was made the vehicle of the author's meditations on the deepest problems of life and mind. Some biographers write to amuse; for Morley biography was an instrument of moral influence. Many a young reader of Morley's biographical work has been affected in his outlook upon life by these noble, ripe, and well-balanced volumes.

The phrase 'man of letters' is, then, inadequate to

describe the peculiar quality of Morley's literary contribution. Literature was for him not so much an
end in itself as a means to a further end which was
social, not individual. 'Literature is not only', he
writes, 'a fine art. It is also a practical art.' Again
and again he recurs to the thought that the best
books come from men who have been preserved by
the animating surges of public life from the trivial,
the fastidious, and the academic spirit. The greatest
historians have been soldiers, bankers, statesmen,
men of affairs; the finest moralists those who have
experienced in their own lives the abrupt and awkward turns of fortune, and so in an age which was rich
in spiritual leadership, John Morley, though belonging to no sect and standing outside the Churches, and
refusing, despite many ties of sympathy, to be en-
rolled a Comtist, stands among the prophets.

He preached, and what he preached he practised,
the gospel of intellectual courage and responsibility.
His little book on 'Compromise', which was widely
admired and read by thoughtful young men and
women, was an essay on the importance of Truth,
on the necessity of forming correct opinions, on the
obligation which rests upon everybody to defy conventional cant and hypocrisy and contribute as best
he may an independent judgement to the common
stock.

In our English public life there is nothing in the
long run which pays like pluck. John Morley had
pluck. Everybody felt that he was a self-sufficient,
dauntless man, 'captain of his soul', ready to face the

heat and dust, the inflexible champion of his own opinions, however unpopular. He was not afraid to avow his agnosticism in religion or to resist the mounting tide of Imperialism which brought British armies to Khartoum and Pretoria and preferred to lose his seat at Newcastle rather than concede to the clamour for an eight-hours day.

Yet despite temporary setbacks the confidence in him steadily grew. The public felt him to be a man who stood for a coherent body of thought, and was interested in the working of large political principles rather than in the rough and tumble of party politics. He was widely known as 'Honest John'. Despite his bookishness he could talk straight to simple men. From many a platform his strong, musical voice carried the message of a fiery and poetic temperament to the common jury.

He was taunted with being a doctrinaire, but if he was a doctrinaire he was free of the dryness, the pedantry, or the intellectual stiffness which are usually associated with that name. On the contrary, he was the most sensitive and affectionate of men, full of warm, human sympathies, alive to the infinite possibilities of the human destiny, and forward in the great human causes of his time. Nor was his mind closed to lessons of different circumstances. An admiring disciple of Burke, he realized, as any man of action must do, that emergencies must be handled as they arise, and that all history is a choice of evils.

Time cooled the hot animosities of his combative youth. The Court, the House of Commons,

the established Church, ceased to be causes of violent
offence. The responsibilities of office swung the pendulum of his inclination towards the side of authority,
so that as Secretary of State for India he was prepared
to revise his early estimate of Mazzini and to find
merits in the strong hand of government which he had
not surmised in youth. A thorough-going democrat
in England, he resisted the notion that parliamentary
institutions could ever be appropriate to Indian conditions. A Little Englander, however, he remained
to the end, and when the rough clouds of the Great
War blew away and Liberals and Tories alike were
prepared to worship the ark of the Covenant, he expressed dissent, fearing that Britain might be drawn
into a long train of hazardous commitments by the
League.

He was not, and did not aspire to be, a philosopher
in the technical sense of that term. Utilitarianism is
the ethical creed of the man of action, and Morley
was a Utilitarian. In his philosophy of history he
went to Comte, saving that he assigned to Protestantism, and, in particular, to Protestantism in its Cal-
vinistic form, an influence on the political destinies of
mankind for which the French thinker had made no
allowance. His workaday creed was derived from his
master Mill: 'Save the individual; cherish his freedom; respect his growth, leave room for it; abominate
the abuse of power; let reason have fair play; do not
expect of life more than it is capable of bestowing.'
Bacon's fine saying: 'The nobler a soul is the more
objects of compassion it hath' was constantly in his

mind and engraved on his mantelpiece at Flowermead. Commiseration for the outcasts and the downcasts of society lay at the root of his politics. He could see nothing good in war, nothing but a measureless retrogression of society and abasement of moral standards, a free rein to cruelty and barbarism, and an interruption of all beneficial policies.

So his literary criticism bears the stamp, both in its choice of subjects and in its method of approach, of his moral fervour and warm interest in the elevation of the social and intellectual life of man. He admired Mill for his ardent interest in humanity, coupled with his reasoned attention to the law of its conditions; Carlyle for his assault upon the dogmatic temper in religion, and the cant and hypocrisy of the country; Byron for his mastery of revolutionary emotion and sublime sense of the melancholy of history; Voltaire for his hatred of cruelty and obscurantism and brave service to humanity; Rousseau for his reverence for human worth; the *Encyclopaedia* for its social aim, its glorification of human virtues and justice; Victor Hugo as the genius of pity; George Eliot as having given imaginative application to the great influx of new and exciting ideas which spread through England between 1856 and 1876.

If he had not the delicacy of Pater, the psychological penetration of Stephen, or the easy grace of Matthew Arnold, he had all the solidity which he admired so much in Sainte-Beuve, and that sense of direction to large, social and moral ends which he found so stimulating in the talk and in the writings of Mill.

That he was, in a much deeper sense than most professed churchmen, sensitive to the appeal of religion emerges from a beautiful passage in the essay on 'A New Calendar of Great Men' in which, writing of the *Imitatio Christi*, he draws the distinction between Holiness and Virtue:

'We are told that, historically considered, the *Imitatio* is to be viewed as the final summary of the moral wisdom of Catholicism; that it is a picture of man's moral improvement as the first and constant aim for every individual. I do not say that any of this is untrue, but is moral the right word? Is not the sphere of these famous meditations the spiritual rather than the moral life, and their aim the attainment of holiness rather than moral excellence? As, indeed, another writer under the same head better expressed it, is not true inspiration the yearning for perfection, the solution of the life out of self? By holiness do we not mean something different from virtue? It is not the same as duty; still less is it the same as religious belief. It is a name for an inner grace of nature, an instinct of the soul, by which, though knowing of earthly appetites and worldly passions, the spirit purifying itself of these, and independent of all reason, argument, and the fierce struggles of the will, dwells in living, patient and confident communion with the seen and unseen Good. In this region, not in ethics, moves the *Imitatio*.'

It is difficult to do justice to the charm of Morley's conversation, never lapsing into the commonplace, always easy, graceful, shot through with humour, and raising topics which were worth talking about. I never remember being present at a party at which Morley's eager, expressive, challenging interventions did not exalt the general level or strike from others an answering fire. I have heard many good talkers in my life, none more brilliant or witty than my friend Edmund Gosse, but Morley's talk stands out from all other by reason of the fact that over and above its literary quality, its charm of manner and ready sympathy, its playful ease reminding one of a Platonic dialogue, there was always a sense of exploration, a serious proposition to be sustained or examined.

In the art of indicating emphatic dissent from a friend without giving offence or showing any trace of bitterness he was a past master, so that his opponent had some difficulty in discerning, beneath the exquisite courtesy of his sympathetic compliance, what was always below—an impregnable rock of purpose and principle.

An example of this gracious urbanity in circumstances of great emotional disturbance lives in my recollection. One night in the late autumn of 1914 five men sat down to dinner at a London club. Two of them were Morley and Edward Grey, a third was Haldane. After some general conversation on indifferent topics, Morley, who had been visibly chafing under a sense of repression, opened out upon the burning theme which was in all our minds. Why had we gone to war? Why had we not advised Belgium to let the Germans through? How could we justify to posterity the Iliad of woes which this war would bring in its train? For the remainder of the evening we listened to a duel between the two friends, each of them deeply moved by the size and tragedy of the issue, each in deadly earnest, yet in their vigorous exchanges never for a moment forgetting the respect and affection which they entertained for each other. The debate lasted far into the night. As we rose to go, Morley discharged a final shaft: 'And remember, Grey, that there is a little island across St. George's Channel, its wounds unstanched and its wrongs unredressed. After the war you will hear from her.'

Hear from her indeed we did. But even of the Anglo-Irish trouble there came at last an end. And so, bearing that seven-years-old conversation in mind, I hastened to Wimbledon on the morning of the Anglo-Irish Treaty to bring Morley the news. I shall not easily forget the depths of his emotion. After her long and stormy Odyssey the Home Rule ship, battered by wind and waves, had at last been brought to her moorings. Morley was overjoyed, and to mark the occasion he presented the messenger with an inscribed photograph of Victor Hugo which the old French poet had given him in recognition of a review of *Les Travailleurs de la Mer.*

A few days later it fell to him to move the adoption of the Treaty in the House of Lords. The occasion was historic; the red benches were filled to overflowing, and the choice of the orator was universally approved. Though his frame was broken and his voice so feeble that it hardly reached the group which were standing on the steps of the Throne, there was yet enough of the old magic and familiar ardour in his utterance to remind his hearers of the man he had been. We dispersed in satisfaction as after a good night at the play. That it should have been given to the veteran champion of Irish liberty to announce in his last public speech the triumph of the Irish cause was felt to be one of Chance's happy compliments and a graceful close to a tragic tale.

X

AN AUTOBIOGRAPHY BY
PHILIP VISCOUNT SNOWDEN[1]

LORD SNOWDEN'S autobiography has many conspicuous merits. It is clear, able, honest, and
unaffected. It divulges all that the author thinks it
important that the general public should know about
him, and it is very unlikely that the general public
will wish to know more. There are some men who,
like the late Lord Rosebery, will always be a little
mysterious to themselves and a great deal more mysterious to others. Philip Snowden, to call him by the
title by which he is most familiar, is not of this company. He has no secrets to hide, no unruly body of
inner doubts and misgivings to compose behind the
scenes, no apologies to make, no obscurities to clarify,
no delicate half-shades of meaning and intention to
present to the appetite of the psychological virtuoso.
His intellect stands out clear-cut, robust, and confident against the background of his times. His great
strength is that he has always known where he wanted
to go, and that his every action has been grounded
on a good reason.

Another qualification for a biographer Lord Snowden possesses in a high degree. His subject inspires
him with keen entertainment and satisfaction. The

[1] *An Autobiography by Philip Viscount Snowden*, vol. ii.
Ivor Nicholson & Watson. 21s. Reprinted from the *Fortnightly
Review*.

career of a delicate son of a working weaver, born in a poor Yorkshire cottage, and rising by force of energy, character, and ability to be Chancellor of the Exchequer and a Viscount is a theme calculated to stir even the dullest imagination. Lord Snowden may be forgiven if he retraces the story with pride and enthusiasm. He is proud of his admirable father and mother, of the little village in which he was born, of his native county of Yorkshire, the characteristics of which he so fully embodies, and, as he showed to the delight and somewhat to the surprise of the House of Commons in the peroration of his last Budget speech, he is proud also to be an Englishman. Those who have been accustomed to think of him mainly as a demagogue and Parliamentary gladiator with a very bitter tongue, will be surprised to find how rich is his capacity for enjoyment and appreciation. The newspapers have already made copious excerpts from these two volumes which expose their author in his familiar role as an acrimonious and devastating critic. But Lord Snowden is not all East wind, as his friends know. His autobiography abounds in generous tributes, not only to his wife, the valiant and intelligent partner of his labours, but to his old comrades of the Labour Movement, to many political opponents, and noticeably to Mr. Montagu Norman, the Governor of the Bank of England, whose constant solicitude for the economic convalescence of Europe our author learnt to value when he came to administer the finances of the Kingdom from Treasury Chambers. From such passages the reader will gather a fairer impression of

Lord Snowden's true character than that which is ordinarily entertained by those who have never come into personal contact with him.

With all this, Lord Snowden is a born Parliamentarian. It is not difficult for him to treat his Parliamentary opponents as the greatest scoundrels in the world, however much he may like them in private life. Controversy has always been the breath of his nostrils. He enjoys giving, and does not mind receiving hard knocks. His bouts with Mr. Winston Churchill, an opponent worthy of his steel, afforded him huge pleasure at the time, and still, as is evident from these pages, give him pleasure in the recollection. It is obvious that it has been a delight to him to live over once more his Parliamentary triumphs. He bears no malice, for he knows that in every encounter he has given as much as he has received. It was said by one who listened to Robespierre's maiden speech in the National Assembly, 'this man will go far, for he has a foundation of bitterness and eloquence'. Lord Snowden, like Robespierre, has this foundation. His rise to power in the Labour Party was due not only to his gift for clear and cutting speech, but to the religious force of his socialist ideals. He felt the rich to be enemies, and as such assailed them. In a remarkable passage he describes how little he was affected by the teaching of Karl Marx, but how deeply he felt the injustice of an order of things which was compatible with those violent contrasts of luxury and want which are characteristic of English society.

The second volume of the Autobiography, which

takes up the story after the close of the War, lacks the great human interest attaching to the early struggles of the young Labour leader and to the infancy of the Labour Movement. The author is now an elderly statesman, fully conscious of his responsibilities, and intolerant of the wild extremes to which the Left Wing of his Party was prepared to go. On the burning subject of Russian Communism he took up at once a strong stand. When, in April 1920, he was compelled as President of the I.L.P. to preside over a discussion at Glasgow as to whether or not the I.L.P. should join the Moscow international, he made up his mind that if the Conference decided in favour of affiliation with Moscow, he would leave the Chair. Fortunately the Conference turned down the proposal. Lord Snowden then remained President, using his intellectual weight against the Russophile Communists. 'My quarrel with the Communists', he writes, 'is not so much with Communism as a thing, as with the methods by which they seek to establish a Communistic State. . . . No social system will ever endure which is based on class antagonism and upon hatred and selfishness.'

These excellent doctrines were far from being the common property of the Labour Party during the troubled years which succeeded the War. In the excitement generated by the proletarian victory in Russia, many minds felt the attraction of the General Strike as a weapon wherewith a Parliamentary Government might be brought to heel. Even Lord Snowden went so far as to join with Mr. Thomas and Mr. Clynes in threatening the Government with a General Strike in August 1920, when it was feared that Mr. Lloyd George might be tempted to help in the defence of Poland against the Bolsheviks.

That was a very dangerous line to take. Lord Snowden, however, defends it, though, as a matter of fact, there was never the faintest possibility of the Cabinet sanctioning a new war for the defence of the Poles.

When the General Strike did come in the end the moderate Labour leaders found themselves placed in a position of great difficulty. They never believed in the strike, but on the other hand they felt that they would lose their influence over the rank and file of their party if they capitulated to the Government. Lord Snowden was, of course, far too sensible a man to expect that any good would result from this madcap proceeding. When the crash came he remained silent for nine days, secretly glad that the experiment had failed since the Trade Unions needed a lesson of the futility and foolishness of such a trial of strength.

It will be seen that Lord Snowden, though steadily professing the philosophy of the Socialist, was in fact an old-fashioned Free Trade radical. When Labour first took office, he was in favour of friendly relations with the Liberals. 'Looking back on the nine months' life of the Labour Government, I am forced to the conclusion that both Parties pursued a policy which was more resembling a lot of irresponsible children than of responsible statesmen.' No doubt there were faults of temper on both sides; but the real difficulty is passed over by Lord Snowden. All the time that the Liberal members were supporting the Labour Government by their votes, Labour candidates were attacking Liberal seats in the constituencies. The difficulty of establishing any real and continuous harmony between two independent parties in the House without an arranged truce in the constituencies was never more clearly illustrated.

The story of the three Cabinets in which Lord Snowden served, of his budget speeches, and of his relations to his colleagues is told in this volume with great clarity and with little reserve. In general outline the tale is already familiar, for this is an age of Cabinet indiscretions; but Lord Snowden adds, from his personal experience, some piquant and not always very charitable reflections upon Mr. MacDonald and others with whom he was associated at this time. He is right, however, in pointing out that Mr. Ramsay MacDonald quite gratuitously threw away the life of the First Labour Government by refusing to entertain the Liberal proposal for a select Committee to inquire into the Campbell Case. Nor in the special circumstances of the case can he be blamed for disclosing to the House of Commons and to the country the full extent of the economies to which Mr. Henderson and his followers in the second MacDonald Cabinet were prepared to submit, when the sharp challenge to instant retrenchment came from the banks in 1931. Indeed, there can be little question but that Lord Snowden's vigorous speeches in Parliament and over the wireless exercised a great influence in securing for the National Government its mammoth majority. An old-fashioned reader of these entertaining volumes may ask himself whether he is really entitled to be taken so much behind the scenes. The old rule used to be that what passed in the Cabinet did not go outside, and that it was contrary to public policy to repeat the private conversations of Cabinet colleagues on public affairs. In the interests of ministerial cohesion and the effective conduct of Cabinet business, there is everything to be said for this convention. Of late the rule has been relaxed. No doubt a special case can be made for full disclosures relative to the conduct of the War in view of the poignant interest which the War must necessarily excite in the minds of the generation which lived through it. The circumstances, also, which led to the formation of the first National Government clearly belong to a special category. But I am old-fashioned enough to hope that in future the old convention of Cabinet secrecy will be restored, and that the custom of smoking at morning cabinets (introduced under the first Labour Government) will be put down with a high hand.

XI

A. J. B.[1]

I DOUBT whether any British Statesman has lived a fuller, happier, or more fortunate life than Lord Balfour. Few of the gifts which mortals envy were denied him. He had wealth and station, brains and good looks, a philosophic temper, and a melodious voice. Affection and admiration attended him throughout his brilliant course. If he never married, he was the perfect uncle, entering with affectionate zest into the concerns of the younger members of his clan, and by them regarded as the best, the kindest, and the most understanding of friends. For two generations there was no more dazzling figure in London Society than this tall, beautiful, gifted bachelor, so gracious in his manner, so formidable in debate, so alert to enter into any human interest. Two gifts, each ministering to the highest kind of human satisfaction, were vouchsafed him. He took a passionate delight in good music, and in the delicacies of philosophical and scientific discussion.

A political career is never smooth, and A. J. B., as his friends called him, had his share of reverses, for not only did he lead his party to a great electoral defeat in 1906, but he had four years later the mortification to be superseded in its leadership by a younger and less distinguished man. Yet these setbacks, which might have soured a smaller nature, made little im-

[1] *Chapters of Autobiography*, ed. Blanche E. Dugdale. *Saturday Review of Literature*, Dec. 6, 1930.

pression on A. J. B. As one of his friends said,
'A. J. B. never forgets that we live between one ice age
and another.' In the large context of astronomical and
geological time the ups and downs of the political
game may be viewed with a spirit of detachment, a
speck in that long history of the human race, which
may still have, as the astronomers tell us, a hundred
and fifty thousand million years to run. Besides, for
A. J. B. there was music, and there were games. More
especially games. Until he was nearly eighty he played
golf and lawn-tennis with the zest of a boy, and happy
athletic memories, visiting him during his last illness
have inspired some pages of the autobiographical
fragment which we owe to the pious labours of Mrs.
Dugdale, his niece.

Mr. Lloyd George once said to me, 'Balfour is not
an aristocrat, he is an intellectual'. The distinction is
just. A. J. B. had all the advantages of the aristocrat.
His background was aristocratic, beautiful country
places like Whittinghame and Hatfield, intimate associations with the wealthy and well born, and a fortune
which shielded him from the ugly things and disagreeable expedients of the common life. It was said,
for instance, that he had never travelled in a bus, and
only once condescended to the 'tube' or underground
railway. But though he had the manners of a *grand
seigneur* of the eighteenth century, it was always intelligence which counted with him. He sought out the
society of learned and clever men, and delighted in
their converse.

A first-class autobiography is perhaps hardly to be

expected from a spirit moving in these serene elevations. Though A. J. B. had mixed in great affairs all his life (his first big public experience was the Congress of Berlin in 1878), seen every one worth seeing, and probably heard as much brilliant talk as any man in Europe, his commemorative instinct, more especially in the small, amusing things of life, was never strong. When a man is engaged in high politics, and passionately interested in the world around him, he has little time or taste for commemoration. A. J. B. describes himself to his niece as 'a very lazy man, who has always had a job on hand'. As a matter of fact, he worked very hard, though his uncanny gift of pouncing on the essential point in an intricate argument or situation gave him an unfair advantage over slower minds. But he had no interest in retailing gossip, no verbal memory for quotations, and was far too fastidious to indulge in indiscretions at the expense of his friends. It might therefore have been predicted in advance that an autobiography of Lord Balfour, however full of serious interest for the historian, would be lacking in those lighter and more frivolous elements which the common reader has learnt to expect from this type of literature.

I imagine also that the ideal biographer must be endowed with a spice of personal vanity, or in any case, must be thoroughly interested in himself. Now A. J. B. was not, as I surmise, greatly interested in himself. He was interested in science and philosophy, in religion and politics, in the prosperity of the British Empire, in the happiness and well being of his wide

circle of relations and friends, but not to any large
extent in himself. He would never have kept a diary
of intimate self-scrutiny like Amiel, or contemplated
self-revelations on the scale of Rousseau. The duties
of a patriot, the pleasures of an athlete, the interests
of a philosopher, left him little leisure or appetite
for self-contemplation.

Nevertheless the complete autobiography of a
statesman so long prominent in great affairs would
have been one of the most important historical documents of our age. Unfortunately, the chapters of autobiography, which we owe to the valued labours of
Mrs. Dugdale, are far from covering the whole ground
of Lord Balfour's long life. Hardly had the volume
been launched before Lord Balfour, who was nearing
his eightieth year, was overtaken by the illness from
which he never recovered, and thereafter it was dic-
tated from bed by an invalid whose powers were
steadily ebbing. Save for a few concluding fragments
relating to the author's visit to the United States in
1917, the narrative closes in 1886, before he had
received any office under the Crown.

It follows that much of the autobiography relates
to an episode in the political history of England
which has ceased to possess any general interest.
The manœuvres of the Fourth Party, a little group of
independent Conservative members of Parliament,
who came to the front between 1880 and 1885, provide
no doubt some entertainment to those who are curious
about the minutiae of British Parliamentary history;
and to the understanding of this episode of the past

Lord Balfour makes a brilliant and authoritative contribution. But when we consider the great themes upon which he might have disserted—the Irish Secretaryship, the formation of the Entente with France, the War and the Peace, the American Mission and the League of Nations, how gladly would we exchange the two chapters on the Fourth Party for some leaves taken from the later and more important period of his life! But alas! Lord Balfour's chronicle was all too late begun, and all too soon closed by a sentence from which there is no appeal.

Let us, however, be grateful for what has been given us, and more particularly for the graphic sketch of the intellectual influences which helped to fashion the mind of the future statesman. One of these will not surprise the reader. It was the essays of Macaulay. The other was the conversation of that remarkable scholar and philosopher Professor Henry Sidgwick, whom Balfour met first at the high table of Trinity College, Cambridge, and who was afterwards married to Balfour's sister.

'One day my mother presented me with the posthumous volumes of Lord Macaulay's miscellaneous writings then recently published. Who is there, in these days, who would admit that at any period of his life his intellectual development had been profoundly stimulated by the writings of Lord Macaulay? To be sure no one denies their brilliancy. But, says the critic, brilliancy is but a surface quality, and the antithetical glitter of their style cannot conceal an essential shallowness of insight, a congenital incapacity for philosophic speculation, which must always keep their author in the second rank of nineteenth-century writers. On this point I dare offer no opinion, if only because I am not an impartial judge. My personal feelings are too deeply concerned. For no sooner was I acquainted with these specimens of his writings than I became his fascinated admirer. His style delighted me. I thought his dialectics irresistible. His gifts of narrative carried me away; the things he wrote about invariably interested me; in short, he supplied much of the mental nourishment I desired, in the exact form that best suited my very youthful appetite.'

Sidgwick was probably even more congenial, because he possessed the quality, greatly valued by A. J. B., of being entirely free from dogma.

'In him I found one who, by accomplishments and temperament, was ideally qualified to give me exactly what I needed, exactly in the way I most needed it. He had great knowledge and no dogma. Though an admirable scholar, he never exaggerated the importance of pure scholarship, either in its relation to culture in general, or to philosophy in particular. He was as reluctant as his pupil to regard the intensive study of ancient speculations as the proper prelude to all modern research.'

It is not my present purpose, nor am I competent for the task, to discuss Lord Balfour's contributions to philosophy. Two things, however, may be said of them. In the first place, they are models of simple, perspicuous English. In the second place, they are all governed by the idea that the aesthetic and moral values which give nobility to life cannot be explained by any rationalistic philosophy, but postulate a spiritual principle in the Universe.

It is, however, as a Parliamentarian, and more particularly as a debater in the House of Commons, that

A. J. B. made his reputation. And this, in spite of a defect which he thus describes.

'It has been a serious misfortune to me that, throughout a lifetime largely occupied in public speaking, my want of verbal memory has always made verbal preparation impossible. Randolph Churchill could repeat a column of *The Times* after a single perusal; if, therefore, he had time to write his words, he could secure without difficulty whatever degree of verbal finish he thought desirable. Bonar Law, smoking comfortably in his arm-chair, could compose a speech involving the most complicated arguments and figures without putting pen to paper; and having done so, could use it, in whole or in part, without misplacing a word. I never could discover merely by listening, whether Lord Oxford (Asquith) was speaking impromptu, was repeating from memory, or was reading from a manuscript. Always the right word came, and always without an effort. This, unfortunately, has never been my case. After more than half a century of speech-making there still remains a lamentable difference between my written and my spoken word—a difference not the less lamentable because some of my friends profess themselves quite unable to detect it.'

And yet this passage taken above would give quite an unfair impression of his oratorical powers. When deeply moved he spoke, albeit without notes or verbal preparation, with splendid force, and in flawless English, thinking as he went along, and developing his theme under the glow of a powerful imagination in such a way as to stamp it upon the minds of his audience. Friends have told me that his gifts as a speaker were never more effectively displayed than during the momentous visit to the United States in

1917, which is described in the concluding chapter
of this book, unless it be on that important occasion in
1920, when, rising immediately after Mr. Hughes had
made his proposal for a limitation in the size of battle-
ships, he accepted in tones of moving eloquence the
offer of the American Government, which led to the
Naval Convention of Washington.

Let this article conclude with Lord Balfour's vale-
diction.

'I am as familiar as most public men with contact with
great crowds deeply moved by great events, but nowhere have
I seen, and never had I imagined, anything like the spectacle
presented by our landing in New York, and during our long
slow drive up the long narrow route. There is no city in the
world like New York. It was exactly like going through a
canyon whose prodigious walls were pierced with tier above
tier of windows, and every window crowded with heads and
waving handkerchiefs. It was a most impressive experience.
This memorable day concluded with a great banquet given
in the Hotel Astoria to the French and British Delegates. I
was under the guidance of my old friend, Mr. Choate,
formerly American Ambassador at St. James's. I had driven
with him to service in the Anglican Cathedral. As I parted
with him on the steps we took a tender farewell of one
another, for I was returning to Washington that night. As
we shook hands he said, "We probably shall not meet again
till peace is reached". He was right. He died within a few
hours from heart failure.'

XII

A PHILOSOPHER'S PARADISE

M<small>R. BERTRAND RUSSELL</small>,[1] enjoying the luxuries of a
philosopher, plots a world state organized on
a Communist basis. There is no religion, unless the
Communist Faith can be so called, there are no
churches, no armies, no social classes, and, of course,
no capitalists. The British Empire, which has been the
object of so much foolish and unfortunate applause,
is wiped off the slate together with the Public Schools,
which have hitherto helped to sustain this deplorable
fabric. Every element in our present civilization
ministering to national sentiment is condemned as in
the highest degree deleterious to the best interests of
mankind. Mr. Russell's Paradise is as flat as a pan-
cake.

A change of this order of magnitude will not be
accomplished in the twinkling of an eye. Mr. Russell's
intellectual honesty compels him to admit that during
the period of transformation, which may extend, perhaps, for a century and a half, humanity will be compelled to tolerate 'certain crudities'. One of those
crudities will be war, for Mr. Russell is disposed to
believe that Capitalism, and perhaps the British Empire, will make a fight for it. Nevertheless, the salutary
revolution will, in course of time, be effected. A

[1] *Education and the Social Order*, by Bertrand Russell (Allen
& Unwin, 7s. 6d.). Reprinted from *John O' London's Weekly*,
vol. xxviii, no. 709.

drastic reformation in our educational methods may help it to come swiftly and painlessly, and before the old national system of the world has been ruined by its inherent vices. Meanwhile, even a millionaire may have his uses. He may found a hospital for identical orphan twins, which will enable Science to determine more accurately than has hitherto been found possible the relative influences of heredity and education. On this difficult and obscure subject Mr. Russell refrains from dogmatism. He is merely content to dispose of the aristocratic theories of the Eugenists by pointing out that they are not proven, and having so cleared the ground of a formidable obstacle addresses his ingenious and unconventional mind to the problem of improving the human race through education. Mr. Russell satisfies himself that Education can do a great deal:

'Education could easily, if men chose, produce a sense of the solidarity of the human race, and of the importance of international co-operation. Within a generation, the vehement nationalism from which the world is suffering could be extinguished, the tariff walls by which we are all making ourselves poor could be lowered, the armaments with which we are threatening ourselves with death could be abolished, and the spite with which we are cutting off our own noses could be replaced by goodwill. The nationalism which is now everywhere rampant is mainly a product of the schools, and if it is to be brought to an end, a different spirit must pervade education.'

How is this spirit to be produced? Mr. Russell's prescription involves elements so various and unequal as the following: an historical text-book to be prepared by the League of Nations and the American Government in co-operation with the Soviets for use in all the schools throughout the world, the abolition of all religious teaching, the abolition of all competition, the freedom of children to be dirty from morn to eve, the freedom of children to swear, the freedom of children to be indecent, the freedom of children to be disrespectful to parents, the freedom of children to be absent from their classes, the freedom of children from criticism upon their literary compositions, and the encouragement of companionate, childless marriages among university students.

For some reason, which has been withheld from his readers, Mr. Russell persuades himself that young people so brought up will be more immune from class combativeness, less Imperialistic, and more able to produce the enduring Communist Peace which is to relieve our troubles than the brood which now issues from the schools. 'The mentality of the Imperialist, reinforced by the complexes of the sexually starved', is the dragon which our St. George sets out to destroy. But what is the connexion between sexual starvation and Imperialism? The Japanese have no sexual taboos, as Mr. Russell gratefully acknowledges, and the sexual starvation of the student of the *Quartier Latin* has not yet reached a point which deserves Mr. Russell's commiserating and remedial attention. Nevertheless, France and Japan must be regarded as military, and even as Imperialist, nations. In comparison, the sexually starved youth of Great Britain shine in a halo of civilian virtue.

The temporary, childless marriage, which Mr.
Russell cordially recommends as an expedient calculated to improve the intellectual and moral life of
most university students, is so largely practised on the
continent of Europe with results exactly the reverse of
those which Mr. Russell desires, that, quite apart from
a priori reasons grounded on principles of Ethics,
Religion, and Hygiene, it is never likely to commend
itself to a wise and disinterested counsellor of youth.
That Mr. Russell should recommend it is, of course,
due to the influence of Freud. This able psycholo-
gist, with the tendency of a Teuton pedant to over-
drive a new theory, was tempted to refer most of the
maladies of the soul to the suppression of sexual
emotions in youth. Mr. Russell, whose weakness it
is to take too much from text-books, shares these
opinions, and allows them to discolour his view of the
landscape. So while Mr. Russell's volume is full,
as we should expect, of valuable criticism and of helpful suggestions, as, for instance, that Arithmetic is
generally begun too soon, and that Mathematics are
overvalued in our public elementary schools, we much
doubt whether his general doctrine will find favour
with those who have been most successful in teaching
the young. For instance, it is quite possible, we
imagine, for a small class of intelligent children to be
managed by a staff of intelligent teachers in a way so
stimulating that the vulgar inducements supplied by
competition are unnecessary. Competition, of course,
like all history, is a *pis aller*. It supplies an induce-
ment to exertion, which would not otherwise be

forthcoming. But are we not compelled to assume that many intellects will be sluggish, and that many teachers will be indifferent, and if such assumptions be granted, can we dispense with competition? The idea that school competition breeds bad blood among the competitors either in sport or in the classroom, or that it is the nursing mother of militarism in after-life, seems to be at variance with facts and probabilities.

With that part of Mr. Russell's doctrine which is founded on the desire to protect the weak and the eccentric and to diminish 'the pressure of the herd' in school every humane educator will be in the fullest sympathy. The strength of Mr. Russell's educational philosophy is his abhorrence of brutality, his love of truth, his reverence for reason and knowledge, and his detestation of imposture. His weakness is a tendency to intermix with passages of admirable meditation propositions so violent in form that the modest element of truth which they contain is rendered almost undiscoverable. State and Church have often conspired to suppress intellectual liberty. They have also often united to provide educational opportunities. At no time, probably, in the whole course of the history of the planet, has so much of the educational and scientific progress of the world been due to State provision as in our own age. Yet Mr. Russell observes 'at present, except in Russia, all progress has to be won in opposition to Church and State'. This proposition may be a correct deduction from some general theory which a Communist philosopher is bound in consistency to hold, but it is not a statement to which an historian can give his assent.

Again, if it be true that education in the modern world tends to be a reactionary force, the reason is not, I think, to be found in the sphere of politics or social snobbishness as Mr. Russell maintains. It is not, for instance, true that most educators are 'adherents of the rich'. On the contrary, the vast body of the primary school teachers in Europe, who form, of course, the majority of our educators, are to be found in the parties of the Left and are commonly believed to entertain radical, if not subversive, opinions. What is true is the extraordinary difficulty of recruiting men and women in any large numbers possessed of that wide individual culture without which teaching so easily becomes lifeless and mechanical. The conservatism of education, in a word, is not so much due to the pressure of government or to the social attraction of wealth as to the narrow intellectual limitations of the average teacher and his unwillingness to face the pains of independent thought.

That more weight should be attached to universal history and less to national history as an element in the education of the young is a proposition to which I should myself assent. The serious evil of nationalism, which constitutes such an ever-present menace to the peace of the world, might, one would hope, be reduced by methods of historical teaching calculated to give a juster view of the contributions which other nations have made to the progress of humanity.

World history can be made quite as interesting to

children and much more instructive than national
history. But it is idle to suppose that world history
will carry us very far on the road to universal peace.
The rancour and ill will of certain nations seems to be
ineradicable.

This leads me to the public schools. No one can
object to Mr. Russell's attempt to disturb the dogmatic slumbers of the public schools. But if his object
be the attainment of a better international spirit, is he
altogether well advised to do so? Is it not at least a
tenable proposition that Englishmen educated in these
establishments, however defective on the score of
morals and intellect, are upon the whole of a friendly,
indulgent, forgiving disposition? One day during the
War M. Maurice Barrès, the well-known French
nationalist writer, was staying with me in Oxford,
with a view to collecting material for a work upon the
English military and naval effort. At his desire I spent
a Sunday translating into French a bundle of Oxford
letters written from the trenches. '*Mauvais esprit*',
he observed again and again at any expressions of
friendliness towards our German enemies. The tone
of these young Englishmen greatly pained him. They
had no rancour, no hostility. They were treating the
War with an unworthy levity which in France would
be impossible. The indispensable foundation of international hatred was absent. Yet Mr. Russell, who
desires nothing more than international goodwill,
would make short work of the public schools.

'Orthodoxy is the grave of the intelligence,' says Mr.
Russell. Well now, is it? Mr. Russell's own spelling,

grammar, and English style are impeccably orthodox. It would be difficult to name a writer whose pen more scrupulously conforms itself to the best, the most aristocratic, tradition of English prose. But even Mr. Russell's active intelligence can only practise its challenging scepticism over a limited field. The greater part of his knowledge is accepted without inquiry. The greater part of his conduct conforms to the norm. Mr. Russell does not trouble himself to dispute the date of the Norman Conquest nor the rule of three. He lives in a house, wears clothes, pays taxes, sells his books, and keeps to the rule of the road. It is only his general orthodoxy which gives him the leisure to develop his particular heresies. Without the acceptance on faith of some things, there can be no rational criticism of others. As Mr. Russell himself says admirably in another place, 'Adventurousness and courage are admirable qualities, but they are more easily developed against a background of fundamental security'.

We are therefore less depressed than Mr. Russell appears to be by the contrast between the free, creative play of the individual mind, to which he rightly attaches so much importance, and the repressive, and in some cases reactionary, influences of modern education to which he draws our attention. On the whole the modern world and modern systems of education, as they have been developed in the progressive nations of the West, have provided that background of security against which the courageous and adventurous qualities of the human mind may more easily develop them-

selves. Nobody can pretend that the pace of Science
has been slow. Nobody can allege that the crop of
heresies has been small. Nobody can be confident
that in Communist Russia, as it will emerge after a
century and a half of 'crudities', the conditions will be
more favourable to the free life of the intellect than
they are now in England or France.

Schools are necessary. In an admirable passage
Mr. Russell shows how specially necessary schools
are to the children of the urban poor; and for obvious
practical reasons, such schools, if they are to be
efficient, must be of a certain size. But can we be
certain, is Mr. Russell himself truly certain, that he is
making the world safe for Communism—a system
founded on brotherly love—by enacting that children
should be free to be obscene, insolent, and pugna-
cious, for fear lest the repression of certain emotions
may poison the inner harmony of the soul? Perhaps,
it is unjust to Mr. Russell that the question should
be put in this form, for it is not expressly laid down
in the charter of freedom that the happy little liber-
tine is free to fight. We cannot, however, imagine
that Mr. Russell would abridge the discretion of the
young in a matter to which they are prone to attach a
quite particular importance.

XIII

NAZI IDEOLOGY[1]

IF any one should be feeling too happy about the
world and in need of a good stiff lowering diet,
let him read the remarkable survey of the Nazi
ideology contained in Dr. Aurel Kolnai's *The War
Against the West*. Though Dr. Kolnai belongs to the
persecuted race and makes no secret of his Jewish
connexions, he is sensible enough to realize that
the best way with the persecutor is to allow him to
speak his own mind without let or hindrance. His
lengthy volume is, in fact, little more than a *cento* of
quotations from a long list of Nazi authorities, and
the reader who has had the endurance to persevere
to the end of it will probably ask himself if any chapter
in the history of human thought is more sombre or
forbidding.

Judged by these extracts there now exists in Europe,
it appears, a great nation which has been brought
under the strain of historic events to profess a creed
of unbridled material power, which believes that
morality and reason, pity and love, and every form of
humanitarian sentiment and effort are contemptible,
which exults in war and violence, which renounces
Liberalism in all its forms, spurning such ideas as the
rights of man, freedom of speech, and parliamentary
government, and which finds in a blind obedience

[1] Reprinted from *John O' London's Weekly*, vol. xxxix, no.
1,008. Aug. 5, 1938.

to primitive racial passion its supreme ideal and inspiration.

Between such a creed, if this doctrine may indeed be regarded as the creed of the German people, and the beliefs of the civilized West, there can, in the view of Dr. Kolnai, be no compromise. Tribal selfishness cannot make truce with humanity or objective standards of right and wrong. The tyranny of the totalitarian State has nothing in common with the freedom of parliamentary democracy. A people which glorifies war as the highest form of human activity finds no true point of contact with those who regard the preservation of peace and the cultivation of its arts as among the chief aims of statesmanship. There can be no points of agreement between Satanism, for such in its extreme manifestations the Nazi creed appears to be, and a political philosophy rooted in the Christian traditions of Europe.

Dr. Kolnai therefore concludes that 'the central idea of an understanding with Nazi Germany is fundamentally futile and pointless'; that 'no concession, however large, can succeed in weakening or eventually removing the Nazi menace', and that 'the world of civilization must organize itself against the rebels to mankind'.

Does this doctrine, it will at once be said, lead inevitably to war? Dr. Kolnai holds not. 'An armed conflict', he observes, 'must not be looked upon as a fatal necessity or an unbelievable horror. No war, particularly in a complex situation like this, is simply and strictly inevitable; a preventive war would not produce an integral refutation of Nazism and would leave the deepest moral energies of Western nations unused.'

What, then, is the remedy? Dr. Kolnai sensibly observes there is no such thing as a single remedy; that Nazism must be resisted by every moral, scientific, social, economic, diplomatic, and, if need be, military resource, but that one essential condition of eventually delivering the world from its danger is the establishment of a moral unity between the powers which stand for civilization. That unity would not be confined to the West. 'It would embrace the Slavic East, Soviet Russia, and various other countries and powers which are not primarily Western as well.'

It is, however, a material point to consider how far the German people have really accepted the grotesque and terrible doctrines which are so ruthlessly exposed in this volume. In every people there are many savage natures, and the experience of the War would seem to make it probable that the proportion of savage natures in Germany is comparatively high. On the other hand, it is difficult to believe that the vast majority of the German people are not anxious for peace, or have ceased to cultivate the gentler virtues, or have turned their back upon humanitarianism, or that they would accept as truly representative of their modes of thought many of the atrocious and diabolic sentiments which are contained in the recent writers whom Dr. Kolnai has cited in evidence.

The problem of Europe is how to assist this better but inarticulate and helpless Germany to throw off the hateful elements of the political religion which now imprisons it. A war would bring no improvement. On the contrary, it would make things worse than ever. A self-respecting country refuses to alter its ideals under pressure of foreign war.

No political philosopher, however wild, is wholly out of relation to the experiences and tradition of his people. The Nazi creed does not originate with Hitler but has a long pedigree running back through Houston Chamberlain and Nietzsche to Fichte and Hegel, and ultimately to Herder. The doctrine of the State as Power belongs to Hegel; the idolatry of the German race as predestined to greatness by reason of its purity to Fichte; the cult of primitive barbarism to Wagner; the contempt of the Christian virtues to Nietzsche; the violent anti-Semitism to Houston Chamberlain, or to Lueger and Luderer, the anti-Semites of Vienna. The worship of force has long been characteristic of Prussian policy and Prussian political thought. It was with blood and iron that Bismarck forged the German Empire. As far back as in 1848 that great man saw in English Liberalism the most dangerous, because the most attractive, foe of the military spirit, and determined that Germany should never be united on liberal lines.

Divested of some of its outrageous and shocking features, 'the Third Humanism', as it is sometimes absurdly called, contains much that satisfies the German appetite. Abased by defeat and suddenly robbed of the smashing victory which had been so confidently expected, with the middle classes ruined by the depreciation of the mark, with the Weimar constitution discredited, with the Communists militant and spreading alarm, and the workers thrown out of employment in millions by the American crash, Germany turned with relief to the harsh, violent visionary who, like Moses, appeared at the critical moment to lead his country into the promised land.

Feder described in advance the qualities to be desired in the Leader: 'He must have a somnambulistic feeling of certainty, must be entirely free from all unnecessary constraints or scruples, must know the art of hating. In pursuit of his aims he must not refrain even from bloodshed and war.'

Adolf Hitler filled these requirements. His Brown-shirt ruffians cleared the streets of the Communists. His obsequious murderers carried out the hideous butchery of June 30, 1934. He put down the Weimar parliament, abolished the sovereign states and the Trade Unions, marched Germany out of the League, tore up the treaties of Locarno and Versailles, established conscription, fortified the Rhineland, annexed Austria, and centralizing German power as it has never been centralized before, cleared the decks for the 'total war'. In a few years he lifted his people from the deepest pit of abasement to a pinnacle of hope and pride. It is not surprising that some authors cited by Dr. Kolnai speak in their excitement of a 'Copernican revolution'. The new religion, however, is no revolution but 'the old dog in a new doublet'. Pan-German ambitions again swing the German mind, and among the desperadoes of the Nazi movement the mad challenge, 'Weltmacht oder Niedergang', 'World-power or Downfall', rings out, as once before on the eve of war.

In all this development much is to be ascribed to the fanaticism and inexperience of youth. The young men and maidens who roamed the country together during the first decade of the peace felt their way instinctively into the Nazi creed. The intricate deliberations of Weimar had no interest for them. They were in quest of a hero. They had little knowledge and much enthusiasm, little gift of self-scrutiny and much power of self-dedication, a lively sense of injuries received from wicked enemies and a hearty wish to avenge them. The front-line man became a demi-god, the Jew, as ever in German history, the scapegoat of national misfortune. As moral inhibitions were flung to the winds, so the wild forces of primitive nature were exalted. The astute Dr. Goebbels saw clearly how much the Hitler movement must depend on the romantic enthusiasm of boys and girls. 'Youth', he observed, 'is always right. For it every "aye" and "no" is not fraught with a "but" and "however".'

The cult of life as such is, therefore, the recurrent theme of Nazi teaching. An education which aims at morality sins against life: 'We no longer believe that reason controls life. We have realized that life controls reason. Life has no goal. Mankind has no goal; we witness the sublime aimlessness of a great performance.' This note of cynical recklessness is characteristic, not of all, but of much Nazi thinking. Some writers even take pleasure from the thought of Armageddon. Ludvig Klages, the High Priest of Vitalism, is one of these cheerful gentlemen. 'We work', he observes with refreshing candour, 'for the extinction of mankind as soon as possible'. So great is his passion for the primitive that he looks forward to the time when 'the roar of the forest will sound again rejuvenated'.

For all these thinkers the main objects of fear and hate are Christianity and Liberalism. Christianity, of course, for how indeed could the figure of the founder of Christianity fail to offer an embarrassing problem to the anti-Semite militarist? Some Nazis frankly regard him as beyond the pale; others persuade themselves that the Galileans were Galatians, that the Galatians were Germans, and that consequently Jesus was not a Jew. Others again, like Rosenberg, are prepared to tolerate the Anointed One on terms despite his non-Aryan ancestry. 'Our image of Jesus must', observes this author, 'be revised. The crucified pacifist must yield to an educating spirit of fire, to a hero.'

Liberalism makes a good Nazi equally uncomfortable. 'Happiness, liberty, equality, the rights of man, progress, these are phantoms soaked in chaos.' Moeller-Bruck sings much the same tune. 'Primitive races have no liberalism. It is through liberalism that races perish.' A horror of public discussion, an unreserved submission of the will to the National leader, are characteristic notes of this new idolatry.

Judged by intellectual and moral tests such a religion has every shortcoming, but we cannot dismiss the creed of the ruling caste in a powerful nation as

unimportant. The Nazi cult of barbaric power arms
policy and shapes event. That is why, humane and
peace-loving as we believe the main body of the
German people to be, these beast of prey doctrines
must create serious misgivings. The new Evangel
cannot be dismissed as a mere academic exercise.
The long and terrible tale of Austrian suicides is the
last grim commentary on its practical working.

The rugged force and sincerity of Dr. Kolnai's
indignant volume must impress any open-minded
reader. The proscription of the German and Austrian
Jews by the Nazis is a shameful page in history, as
shameful as the British participation in the Slave
Trade. We are reminded, however, by Mr. Wickham
Steed, who acts as sponsor to this book, that most of
the Nazi writings analysed by the author were published after 1934 and may therefore be regarded as the
product of a very recent and violent social convulsion.
May we not, then, hope that we are here confronted
by a morbid and abnormal manifestation of the
German mind, which in time may cede to saner influences? How and when those influences will prevail
we cannot say. But sooner or later, somehow or other
Germany must be reclaimed for civilization if Europe
is to escape chaos. It may be doubted, however,
whether 'a moral unity against the rebels to mankind'
in which the Dictator of the Kremlin joins hands
with the Western Democracies is the most promising
avenue to that desirable, and indeed necessary, end.

XIV

POLITICIANS[1]

I REMEMBER reading in one of Mr. Birrell's early
speeches that we must take what we can get, and if
our Generals do not run away and our salaried politicians do not take bribes, that is all we can expect. That
modest aspiration is a useful warning against great
expectations, but so far as the politicians are concerned
I doubt whether the warning is very necessary now,
for there is no class of man more handsomely depre-
ciated by those who are happy enough to follow the
sheltered professions.

The business of a politician is to be concerned with
affairs of State, an honourable, though it may be a
laborious and irksome, occupation. Indeed, rightly
conceived, what calling could be more calculated to
develop all that is best in a man than the task of con-
tributing, either by criticism or construction, to the
government of a country or an Empire? High courage,
swift decision, accurate judgement, clear expression,
the fertile combination of pliancy and principle, the
gift of social compunction and of equanimity under
the disappointments and reverses of fortune associated
with political life—all these endowments are required
of those who desire to reach and to retain a position of
political leadership.

Why, then, do we so often depreciate politicians?

[1] Reprinted from *The Teachers' World*, vol. xxxiii, no. 1108.
Aug. 12, 1925.

Partly, no doubt, because the politician leads a very controversial life; partly because, living in the open, he is every man's mark, and since his is not a business which conduces to depth or originality of thought, he necessarily exposes an easy surface for criticism, partly because he is often suspected of sacrificing his convictions to secure votes.

We must not expect too much of politicians. We must not expect them to be poets. 'No poet', observes Lord Rosebery, 'is a politician, and no politician is a poet. A politician is never so fortunate as to be a poet, and a poet is never so unfortunate as to be a politician.' A poet may have political views. Dante and Milton had very strong political views. So, too, had William Morris and Algernon Swinburne and Coventry Patmore. But to hold political opinions is one thing and to be a politician is another. Some of the most vehement professors of political opinion are a thousand miles removed from being adapted to a life of political action.

Nor is the politician habitually a prophet. History is full of the mistaken prophecies of statesmen. Almost every war has been misjudged in advance: our leading political experts never even to the eleventh hour expected the unification of Germany, or the triumph of Germany in the Franco-Prussian War. The prophecies which have been so confidently made in debate as to the inevitable results of successive extensions of the franchise have invariably been contradicted by the facts. Even Education Ministers are not infallible, for we remember that W. E. Forster, the author of the Education Act of 1870, confidently predicted that the education rate would never rise above 3*d*. in the £. Eloquence is, no doubt, a valuable gift, but it is not necessary for political success. The business of the politician is to say easily intelligible things in a thoroughly clear and unmistakable way. He must not be too superior; he must not have unusual opinions; he will best succeed if he is able to devote extraordinary abilities to the propagation of commonplace views, and since he is called upon to speak very often he cannot always expect to speak very well. Max Beerbohm has argued in an amusing essay that eloquence in the House of Commons is intentionally bad. Nobody, he thought, could speak so ill if he had not made an art of speaking ill. The Hon. Members who shuffle and stumble through their speeches abounding in platitudes and well-worn expressions, and taking half a dozen words to say what could be said in one, are not quite so stupid as they may appear to their audience in the Public Gallery. They are out for business; they have to make their points. Their function is not to carry flame, but weight—to persuade their fellow members that they know what they are talking about, and that they are earnest and honest. A shower of false witticisms, an extravagant brilliance, will not do this. As between studious cleverness and studious dullness it is always safer to be dull.

Those of you who have read Jane Austen's *Mansfield Park* will remember that Lady Bertram 'rather shone in the epistolary line, having early in her marriage, from want of other employment and the circumstance of Sir Thomas being in Parliament, got into the way of making and keeping correspondents, and formed for herself a very creditable, commonplace, amplifying style'. Now, Lady Bertram had clearly the root of the matter in her. In these days of lady members her 'creditable, commonplace, amplifying style' would have brought her to the front, for to have these things is the essence of parliamentary language, which ought to be, and generally, let us hope, is, creditable, which fails of its mark if it is not commonplace, and which should certainly be amplifying, for unless the points are magnified, how can they be made conspicuous?

Now, Lady Bertram was not an exciting person. On a great parliamentary occasion she would have fallen short, but her soothing manner, with that 'creditable, commonplace, amplifying style of hers', would have steered many a little Bill through Committee.

The public is apt to judge politics by the House of Commons. If the debates of the House are dull, it is said that politics are dull. How often do we not hear the Parliaments of to-day contrasted unfavourably with the Parliaments in the days of Fox and Pitt and Burke? This is, I believe, a complete delusion. There may not at the present moment be a publicist so eminent as Burke, or an orator so brilliant as Fox. But the general average is very much higher: the speeches are more practical and better informed, and for one member who took an active part in parliamentary discussions in the days of Charles James Fox there must be now twenty. Pompous eloquence is out of fashion. The kind of speech to which our legislators like to listen is such as the shareholders of a company expect of the chairman of the board.

I think also that without vainglory we may contrast the politicians of to-day favourably both in respect of private and public morals with the politicians who flourished in the days of Mr. Pitt and Mr. Creevey. It will be remembered that Mr. Gladstone was once asked how it was possible for Mr. Pitt to deliver a great oration after drinking three bottles of port. 'You must remember', replied the sagacious statesman, 'that he was addressing an assembly, very few members of which had consumed less.'

Visitors to the House of Commons are, I think, often disappointed to find that the proceedings are in general so prosaic: they expect vivid little incidents—a row, a sequence of eloquent speeches from Front Bench Members, a scene of passionate emotion and great spectacular effect, and they look down upon the number of elderly gentlemen quietly discussing the technical details of a Bill in Committee. The newspapers, which naturally desire to give prominence to disorderly scenes, however unimportant, create an impression upon the public mind that they are necessary incidents of the parliamentary week: in reality, however, the House is a very good business body, possibly the best in the world, and the amount of parliamentary time which is actually wasted in obstruction or trivialities is comparatively small.

In every popular assembly there are certain members who confound notoriety and fame. In one of Miss Edgeworth's novels a prudent mother says to her daughter: 'Elizabeth, you can never be pretty; you had better be odd.' So, too, there will always be members who think that since they cannot be eloquent they had better be noisy; since they cannot be circumspect they had better be confident, and since they cannot go unnoticed they had better be odd. It is more comforting to human vanity to attract attention by eccentricity than to go unmarked, and I do not see why we should complain, since a good deal of pleasure is given in one quarter, and nobody is a penny the worse.

A great American financier said to me a few months ago: 'We do not need politics in the United States, and therefore we do not understand them.' In the arts of party management and party discipline we have little to learn from our American cousins, with whom politics is very much more of a distinct profession than it is with us, but in a large sense it is true that society in the United States is unpolitical. The ordinary citizen is little interested in political questions. He is too busy attending to his private affairs to follow with attention the complicated operations of the State and Federal Governments. Occasionally, when some special turpitude is revealed in the Government of his city or his State, or when a great issue is put before the Federal electorate, he wakes up, takes a vigorous hand in the game—but not for very long. The United States, then, may be a democracy, but it is an intermittent democracy. It is so affluent, so happily sheltered

by size and distance from external attack that it can
afford to neglect politics to an extent which would be
dangerous in Europe. It is only on the occasion of a
presidential election that the whole people become
actively interested in a great public decision. Then
in every home a discussion arises as to the right man
to send to the White House. And, though he may not
go deeply into political issues, the average citizen,
male or female, forms a pretty shrewd estimate of the
characters of the rival candidates.

Moreover, though the average elector in the United
States is ordinarily too busy to be a politician, he is apt
to be possessed of the sound political instincts which
come from a tradition of popular self-government.

He reverences the Head of the State and sees to
it that in every case he is a man whose personal character stands examination. And though he often allows
things to get very bad, there is a point beyond which
he would instantly revolt and insist upon a radical
change of government. Burke said, as you will remember, that the price of liberty is eternal vigilance. The
American voter cannot be said to be eternally vigilant.
He is, on the contrary, constantly offering the blind
eye to blemishes which it is his duty to remove. And
the result is that a large and lusty family of abuses
flourishes under the roof-tree of liberty; but there is
always a social conscience in the background. When
the moral reserves of the nation are called out they
work with surprising and volcanic energy.

If America is unpolitical, how much more so is that
other vast republican federation which spreads from

the Baltic to the Behring Straits—Russia. 'The Russian peasant', it is said, 'has two fleas, a red flea and a white flea, and he is too busy to scratch either'. The recent history of Russia is a lesson on the importance of politicians. No country with a sound political education could have fallen so low or thrown away such splendid advantages: but the Tsarist tyranny educated no politicians, and when the defeated Tsarist armies threw themselves in a paroxysm of rage and lust upon the helpless body of their country, a small body of doctrinaire Communists, inspired by an exploded mid-Victorian philosophy, aided by army deserters, and employing the traditional Tsarist weapon of a secret and tyrannical police, erected a new despotism in the heart of chaos.

Russia is an example of a country which has suffered from a lack of politicians. Ireland affords a contrary proof of an island which has been tortured by too much politics, a plethora of political anxiety and self-scrutiny. Where everybody thinks about politics, and thinks very quickly and brilliantly and passionately about politics, so that to-day's panacea becomes to-morrow's abhorrence, and every public reputation is a mist enthroned on a rainbow, the problem of politics becomes a malady, an obsession. Instead of being a game, a serious interest, it is a fever, 'fretting the body to decay', and filling the mind with images of melancholy sentiment and unending regret.

Prince Bülow in a famous passage described his fellow countrymen as 'political asses'. That is an incivility permissible only to compatriots: but it is clear that at a most critical period of their history the Germans suffered from a marked insufficiency of political common sense. When Mr. Joseph Chamberlain, in all good faith, offered them the right hand of Great Britain, the German people refused it in scorn. The popular delusions about this country as the necessary enemy were so powerful as to upset any statesman who should frame his course on the hypothesis of Anglo-German friendship. And later on the sensible German politicians were never strong enough to stand up against the General Staff. Their most famous and calamitous defiance of the elementary counsels of good sense was the adoption of the unrestricted U-boat campaign, a course which infallibly brought the Americans into the War.

There is a widespread impression that when a war breaks out the politician becomes superfluous. *Inter arma silent leges*, was an old Roman saying. It is true that any wholesome and patriotic country, embarked upon a war, sends its party animosities to sleep, and makes a vigorous endeavour to think in unison on problems of national defence: but a large number of laws are needed to turn a country from a peace basis on to a war basis and back again, and as for the politicians they are never more necessary. *La guerre est une chose trop sérieuse pour qu'on la laisse aux militaires*, said M. Briand, and nothing can be more true. There are no purely military or naval problems. All questions of offence and defence in war are apt to raise political, moral, and economic issues: and even on the mere purely technical aspects of war the statesman is often called in to arbitrate between rival schools of military or naval opinion. It would be interesting to make a catalogue of the important decisions as to war finance, war material, war strategy, and even as to war operations which were taken by Mr. Asquith and by Mr. Lloyd George, and the ministers associated with them. It would not be a short or unimpressive list.

In great national wars the courage of a country is largely kept up by its statesmen. The soldiers and sailors go about their tasks in silence. It is the business of the leading statesmen, with the aid of the Press, to maintain the faith of the people in the justice of their cause, and in its ultimate triumph. In this respect Britain was far better served than her antagonists in the late war. There were no such speeches in Germany as those in which Mr. Asquith unfolded the case of the Allies during the first year of the war, or as those in which Mr. Lloyd George appealed again and again for fresh efforts and exertions. And so, when the autumn of 1918 came the home front suddenly broke in Germany. A complete capitulation was signed in spite of the fact that German armies stood on enemy soil and that hardly a heavy gun had been captured by the Allies during the retreat. Rarely has there been witnessed so swift and sudden a moral débâcle in spite of a military situation which, though serious, was by no means desperate.

In this country the task of legislation is taken seriously. Bills are intended to pass, and are passed to be administered. The criticism on a Bill is generally acute and sustained, and it is seldom that a really weak

point escapes detection. In this respect the British
Parliament challenges a favourable comparison with
the American Congress, which thinks nothing of passing 25,000 Bills in a session, most of them private Bills
giving pensions to individuals, and many of them
never destined to be administered at all. The question
asked at Westminster of a Bill is not, 'Are you beautiful?' but 'Can you work?' Much of the social legislation which is passed on the other side of the Atlantic
is too showy for the drudgery of our imperfect sub-
lunary world. This is why legislative comparisons
between ourselves and our Transatlantic cousins are
never as instructive as they should be. There is a
Speaker in the House of Representatives at Washington and a Speaker in the House of Commons at Westminster. The titles are the same; some of the functions
are identical, but when I saw Mr. Joe Cannon presiding over the House of Representatives he was picking
his teeth, his leg carelessly thrown over the arm of the
Speaker's chair, a red flower in his buttonhole, his
waistcoat unbuttoned, as he chatted to a friend while
the members read newspapers, lay at full length or
strolled about, keeping up a noise quite sufficient to
drown the voice of the orator who was speaking into
the ears of a knot of reporters. How unlike Mr.
Speaker Whitley in his full wig and gown. Yet Mr.
Joe Cannon was really the more powerful person; for,
while the British Speaker is debarred from taking an
active part in politics, Joe was in a position to obstruct
most of the measures promoted by the most powerful
President of modern times.

Politics in this country are remarkably clean. There may be men who go into the House of Commons to advance their private ends, but they must be very few. The vast majority of members of the House of Commons are there to promote the most honourable of ambitions—that of rendering service to the public in an honourable way. People talk about the spoils of office. There are in the material sense no such spoils. There can be few people who reach Cabinet rank who could not earn a larger income in other ways, and are not the poorer financially for their exhausting labours. We have, indeed, payment of members. Mr. Snowden, I remember, told an audience that so far as he was concerned his Parliamentary salary went in postage stamps, and that must be a very general experience in the case of members representing large urban constituencies.

All the apprehensions which used to be so freely expressed as to the corruption of Parliament through payment of members have been shown to be ill founded. Parliament was corrupt in the eighteenth century, when it represented the well-to-do classes. It is, thanks rather to the vigilance of public opinion than to any ethical improvement in the race upon which we may congratulate ourselves, remarkably free from corruption now.

There is, however, a comparatively new manifestation in our political life which requires to be watched. The theory of our Constitution is that the member of the House of Commons represents a constituency. He is a local member, the mouthpiece of local grievances,

and where a constituency has a very strong industrial
or social interest he must be prepared to adjust his
views to it. Thus the member for Plymouth must
stand up for the Dockyard; and the member for
Gloucester must conceal his enthusiasm, if he has any,
for vaccination, and nobody can properly represent
a constituency on the East Coast of Scotland who
professes an indifference to fishing. But of late this
local association has been very much relaxed. An in-
creasing proportion of the House is returned by the
influence of organizations which are not purely local
but extend their influence over several constituencies.
Thus the National Union of Teachers and the powerful Trades Unions and the Federation of British
Industries are represented in the House of Commons.
The brewers, the farmers, the miners, the textile
workers have their chosen spokesmen. I do not know
that any figure has been supplied for the salaries which
are paid to Members of Parliament by organizations
which think it worth while to be represented in the
House of Commons, but the total figure must by this
time be considerable, and the sums so paid have clearly
a more important influence in determining the composition of the House of Commons than the small
official salaries which are charged to the Treasury, and
in many cases do little more than cover the postal
expenses of members.

There was a distinguished Liberal who, after dining
with a famous Whig premier, assured his lordship
that he might count on his support on all popular
questions. 'I want men who will support the Govern-

ment on all unpopular questions,' replied the sagacious statesman. A drove of particularly patient oxen travelling obediently through the lobby to the crack of the whip, enduring endless vigils in the dog-days, and keeping together with neither a murmur nor a sudden breakaway even when the guns are out on the grouse moors, that I imagine to be the beatific vision which floats into the dreams of a harassed Prime Minister. But in truth party politics are never quite as mechanical as they seem to be. People will talk about the tyranny of the Cabinet and 'the servile hordes' who troop to the divisions, and an impression is created that modern politics are lifeless and machine-made, and that the last breath has long since exhaled itself from the dying lips of Parliamentary Freedom. There is great exaggeration in all this. Every party is composed of a number of active groups forming and reforming themselves differently with each occasion and exercising differing modes of pressure upon the minister in charge of a Bill. Nor can a minister, however powerful and however loyally served by his majority, afford altogether to disregard a resolute little knot of men who are opposed to any part of his proposals. Four able men, who act together and work hard, can make an impression on any Parliament. They can talk, they can interrupt, they can delay proceedings, they can, if they know the House, rouse all the slumbering prejudices and antipathies of their fellow members against proposals which have in them, as most legislative proposals have, a solid kernel of unpopularity. And every minister works with his eye on

the clock. The Government is always racing against
time, and fears nothing so much as delay. This,
then, gives a minority its chance. Though it cannot,
in the end, beat the Government of the day on a large
point of principle, it can create difficulties sufficient
to impel even the strongest Government to make concessions. Moreover, before a Bill is introduced to the
House, the minister takes stock of the Parliamentary
position. He considers what his own supporters will
stand and what his opponents will stand, and frames
his measure in such a way as seems to him to be likely
to secure for it the largest measure of Parliamentary
support. An experienced House of Commons man,
like the late Mr. Walter Long, could tell in advance
with great nicety how different sections of the House
would regard such-and-such a clause of a Bill and could
measure the opposition which it was likely to provoke.

A Bill, then, is already a series of Parliamentary
compromises before ever it is submitted to Parliament. Departmental officials, the minister himself, the
Government draftsmen, and, in the case of important
measures, a committee of the Cabinet have gone over
the measure clause by clause, deleting, adding, amend-
ing, with a view of ridding the measure of its more
unpopular and unworkable features, and of making it,·
so far as human nature permits, Parliament proof.
Nor is the need for circumspection very much reduced
by the size of the majority which supports the Government of the day. In committees some of the most
formidable criticism often proceeds from the Government side of the House.

A year in the House of Commons is a wonderful education for any one. The whole business of the Empire passes before the member for review, and a man must be lost to all sense of intellectual and moral proportions and devoid of imagination who is not inspired by that august procession of problems, so various, meaning so much for the happiness or misery of the human race, most of them baffling the wit of man, and many of them evoking the image of times very different from ours, and of the shocks and struggles of our ancestors, the romance of which has never entirely died away. An old Member of Parliament once observed that it was never safe, however empty the House, to relax one's efforts, or to speak with negligence, for there were always the visitors in the Galleries, coming, it might be, from every part of the Empire, whose favourable impression was worth the winning.

But what is a more potent source of energy and direction is the thought that in politics much can be done for the service of man. The great ideas which move the world and exalt the character rarely come from the politicians. They come from the poets and thinkers and religious teachers and artists. They are conceived in meditation and in solitude, and imply a self-sufficiency and freedom of mind to which the politician, exposed to the stresses and strains of active life, can never hope to attain. What the politician can do is something different. It is not his business to be original, to give a new mould to society or to human nature, or to make voyages of discovery into the unknown; but, finding a great conflict of interests in society, it is his mission to attempt to harmonize those interests under the idea of justice. It is here that the justification for the existence of a political class is to be found. The politician's mission is to make intelligible the claims of different classes and individuals in the State, and to obtain for them such measure of satisfaction as is consistent with the common weal.

The great statesmen of the world have had a very concrete sense of human realities. They have not lived in a world of abstractions, but have always kept before them the vision of men and women and children, for the most part poor and struggling, and, therefore, quick to feel the inequalities and imperfections of Government. The stuff of which politics is made is in reality very simple—bread, coal, clothing, meat, houses, and land. To help improve the common lot— this is the ambition which makes, and will continue to make, the biggest and most generous men in any society desire to take up politics.

There are degrees of public spirit. There are some people in whom it is instinctive and a form of genius. Thus Bentham at the age of 82 writes: 'Never has it happened to me to witness suffering on the part of any creature, whether of my own species or any other, without experiencing, in some degree or other, a sensation of the like nature in my own nerves.'

And Mr. Gladstone was nervously affected by the success and hardships of others to an astonishing degree. Now the ordinary politician is not gifted in this way. He is not public spirited by instinct, because that is a note of moral genius, but he belongs to a profession whose *raison d'être* is to be public spirited. It is as much his duty to cure the ills of the community as it is the business of the doctor to heal the bodies of the sick. However disagreeable or immoral he may be as an individual, he is enlisted under the banner of the public service, and should be shot as a traitor if he deserts the colours.

It is right, then, that our politicians should be in the limelight, and that what they say and do should be on record. Nobody is obliged to go into politics; but if a man becomes a politician he incurs a responsibility, and is accountable to the public for his public conduct. I do not think that his private life concerns us except in so far as it stands revealed in his political activity. What we have a right to ask of him is that he should postpone private advantage to the common good. We have no right to pry into his domestic affairs, and I wish that these were not so frequently brought before us.

The political life is full of glory and abrupt disappointment. Let me close with a quotation from a speech of Oliver Cromwell, delivered on January 22, 1655, when after the elation of a successful war, the spiritual reaction had begun to manifest itself:

'When I first met you in this room it was, to my apprehension, the hopefullest day that ever mine eyes saw, as to considerations of this world: for I did look at—as wrapt up in you, together with myself, the hopes and the happiness though not of the greatest, yet a very great, and the best people in the world. And truly and unfeignedly I thought so; as a people

that have the highest and clearest profession among them of
the greatest glory, to wit religion; as a people that have been
like other nations, sometimes up and sometimes down in our
possessions in the world, but never so low, but we might
measure with other nations, and as a people that has had a
stamp upon them from God; God, having, as it were, summed
all our former glory and honour in the things that are of glory
to nations in an *epitome*, within these ten or twelve years past,
to that we know one another at home, and are well known
abroad. And if I be not very much mistaken we were assured
—as I, and truly as I believe many others did think—of a
very safe port. . . . But we, and these nations, are for the
present under some disappointment.'

XV

A UNIVERSAL HISTORIAN[1]

'*LA vieille Europe m'ennuie*,' observed Napoleon. The old Europe does not bore Professor Toynbee, to whom all things are exciting, but he is not content with it. He finds it altogether too small. The little continent does not present an intelligible field of study, and cannot be understood without taking into account extra-European factors which are becoming steadily more important. Least of all can we now afford to neglect that outer world which 'Europe has succeeded in bringing into her ambit through the radiation of her culture'. Accordingly Professor Toynbee sets out with a high heart and an indefatigable pen, not indeed to describe, but to account for the whole panorama of human life upon the planet. A universal war has set a fashion in universal histories. Spengler has been busy in Germany. Professor Toynbee, who is every bit as learned as Spengler, and a great deal less fanciful, performs a like office in England. In three brimming and bulky volumes he offers a first instalment of his extended meditations on the history of mankind.

To the discharge of this formidable task our English historian brings a range of qualities not often found in combination. He is brilliant as a scholar and a linguist. He has travelled widely. Beginning life as a

---

[1] *A Study of History*, by Arnold J. Toynbee (3 vols.: Oxford University Press, 1934). Reprinted from *The Nineteenth Century*, December 1934.

classic and an historian of ancient Greece, he has for
many years been a close student of contemporary
politics and in personal association with men of action.
Untrammelled by dogma, he is sensitive to the mystical appeal of religion and legend. A strong vein of
stoical morality leads him to face with courage
the grim chronicle of human violence, and to extract
from his survey some considerations of a generally
consoling nature. Much study has not quenched the
ardour of an enthusiastic temperament. The reader of
Professor Toynbee's volumes is not allowed to forget
that the author sits at the feet of Plato, Lucretius,
and Goethe, and that if he is a scholar he is also a poet
and a moralist, who discerns in the records of the past
a message of encouragement and inspiration to man.

When we speak of civilization we are naturally induced to dwell upon that form of civilization which
is most familiar to us and now so widely affects
human life in every part of the planet. The western-
ization of the world is, however, as Professor Toynbee points out, rather political and economic than
cultural. Child-marriage, with its manifold social
consequences, persists in India, though many an
Indian village has the telephone, the motor omnibus,
and a wireless installation. Moreover, the scientific
knowledge upon which this extraordinary triumph of
material civilization depends is 'perilously esoteric'.
Even in the West the ordinary citizen knows little of
the delicate and complex intellectual processes which
have brought into being the vast apparatus of material
comforts and conveniences which is offered for his

use. It is not, then, of civilization that Professor Toynbee writes, but of civilizations. Of these he discovers twenty-one, some of them, like the Mayas, extinct, others, like the Coptic and the Jewish, surviving in a fossilized state; some unrelated to other forms of civilized society, others like our own Western civilization, which is related, through a universal religion and a wandering of the peoples, to a previous civilization (the Hellenic) which in many respects is different.

It is not, however, every one's privilege to belong to a civilized society. There are some 650 primitive societies—small, no doubt, and feeble, but still cognizable by ethnologists—which have never succeeded in raising themselves into the civilized category. They remain societies of 'sub-men' rather than of men. Why is this? Not, as Professor Toynbee most earnestly and eloquently contends, from any inherent disability of the blood. 'The capacity for civilization', he argues, 'is the universal birthright of mankind.' To this proposition it is, in Professor Toynbee's view, no substantial reply to point out that, so far, the African negro has made no measurable contribution to civilization. The world is yet young. The history of civilized life upon the planet is only 6,000 years old. There is no reason, then, to believe that the African is incapable of organizing for himself a civilized existence. Indeed, the religious life of the negro in America opens out the possibility that the revival of the true spirit of Christianity and its diffusion throughout the world may be the distinctive contribution of this oppressed people, and if so, a sublime revenge for centuries of outrageous wrong.

We do not know how far Professor Toynbee would be induced to push his happy doctrine of 'civilization the universal birthright', for he admits that some physical environments present so serious a challenge to the human physique as to preclude the emergence of a civilized society. There are also some stocks which have degenerated. Purity of race, however, has very little, if anything, to do with excellence or survival value. Pure Nordics are to be found only in Sweden, pure Alpines only in Slovakia, the Cevennes, Sicily, and Brittany; pure Mediterraneans only in Sardinia and Corsica. The great races of the world, the races which have borne the burden of history (the Greeks, the Romans, the French, the English) are mongrel. Nearly half the civilizations have been created by a mixture of races. There is clearly nothing in colour. Some white men are civilized, but not all, for there are the barbarous Ainus of Japan, and the highlanders of Albania, Mexico, and the Caucasus. It will readily, then, be imagined that our historian deals faithfully with the pestilential nonsense of Houston Chamberlain and the modern German racialists. We are reminded, for the further chastening of our pride, that there are those in Asia who think little of our civilization and find it difficult to endure the high animal smell of our European carnivores.

But if race is to be eliminated as a dominant factor in the moulding of civilizations, what remains? At somewhat unnecessary length Professor Toynbee makes the obvious point that environment alone does not supply the answer. Environment is, of course, a factor; but so to an even greater degree is man, and it is in man's relation to his environment that we find the key which unlocks the secret of historical development. Primitive societies become civilizations when man responds to the challenge of his environment, and fall into decay as soon as environment offers a challenge to which man is unable to make an adequate response. There is perhaps nothing very novel in this doctrine, which Professor Toynbee elaborates with a great panoply of erudition fetched from the most distant and recondite quarters, except perhaps the stress which he lays on the moral quality of the challenge. It must be a bracing challenge. If it is not bracing, it will not educate a civilization.

An instance, which might serve to prove the contrary, is the early civilization of Egypt, which historians, following Herodotus, have been wont to regard as the gift of the Nile. It is, however, contrary to Professor Toynbee's ethical conception of Providence that a great civilization like that of ancient Egypt should arise out of easy physical conditions. The student of Livy hardly needs to be reminded how completely the moral fibre of Hannibal's army was relaxed by the luxuries of Capua. Sentiments culled from the *Agamemnon* of Aeschylus and the *Faust* of Goethe corroborate the moral of the Roman historian. The Nile did not give civilization to the Egyptians: on the contrary, it was only by grim and obdurate labour that the Egyptians wrested civilization from the Nile. So far from being easy, the conditions which confronted the early Egyptians are portrayed as having been tragically difficult—'a terrestrial hell', all jungle swamp and 'howling wilderness'. No doubt we have been tempted in the past to underrate the severity of the challenge presented by the Nile to the makers of ancient Egypt, but, after all, even in those distant days, the Nile had its regular periods of flood and subsidence, and, with the annual contraction of its waters, laid bare a surface of rich soil which, though it may have had to be cleared of reeds and brushwood, afforded, especially on its margins, a remunerative return to labour. It is not, therefore, surprising that the civilization of the Nile valley developed, while civilization in the valley of the Jordan (which, as Professor Edouard Meyer has shown, possesses many points of geographical similarity) did not. The challenge of the Nile was bracing, but the turnover was quick and the profits were good.

The doctrine of challenge and response, once decided on, receives a great number of attractive illustrations at Professor Toynbee's hands. Athens and Sparta, for instance, are confronted by the same challenge. Each of these States is called upon to provide for a redundant population, but whereas Sparta meets her challenge by annexing territory, a process which, since it confronts her with the standing menace of a Messenian revolt, converts her into a puritan and highly militarized State, Athens, led by Solon, turns to international trade, specialized industries, and marine empire. A high degree of civilization was in each of these cases favoured by Nature. She was severe, but not too severe. There is, as Professor Toynbee observes, a golden mean. The Icelanders never flourished in Greenland, and no great thing came out of Aetolia.

Another factor which Professor Toynbee finds to be favourable to human growth is change of scene. The Homeric cycle was the product of migrations. The Norwegians produced their great literature, not in Norway, but in Iceland. The Ottoman and Moghul Empires flourished, not in the central Asiatic home-lands, but in distant territories conquered by force of arms. The Orthodox, or Greek, Church finds most of its votaries, not in Greece, but in Russia. It would, I suppose, also be true to say that the African flourishes nowhere so well as in the island of Jamaica. It may, perhaps, be suggested that Professor Toynbee is apt to lay too much stress on the discipline of hard-ship. It is, no doubt, easy to point out a great number of instances in which geographical difficulties, foreign enmities, and adverse fortunes, or disabling penalties, have evoked human effort and helped to exalt and ennoble the temper of a people. Prussian historians are fond of pointing out the great qualities which were educated by the struggle with the sandy soil of the North German plain and with the numerous enemies who from time to time have invaded a country possess-ing no frontiers other than the bodies of its inhabitants. Nor is any chapter in modern history more impressive than that which describes how the Prussians pulled themselves together after the Napoleonic wars and built up the best civil service in Europe. But is there not something to be said for Aristotle's view that the perfect life postulates as its condition that a man should be sufficiently provided with the necessities to have a mind free for intellectual culture? The growth of civilization surely postulates as one of its conditions the existence of a class of people who are so situated. It postulates an economic surplus, part of which can be spent on the support of a luxurious class, whose new wants are in themselves a condition of the advancement of taste and industry. The mines of Laureion must be worked by slaves that Ictinus may be free to plan the Parthenon. The fact that all through antiquity slavery was regarded as an essential of social organization and that nobody proposed its abolition would seem to point to the fact that there was a stage in human civilization when without some form of compulsory mechanized man-power cities could not be built, or a cultivated class brought into being. The conditions presented to man by his environment were such as to necessitate, or as to appear to necessitate, this response. Certainly a good deal of forced labour must have gone to the making of the civilizations of Babylon and Egypt.

Professor Toynbee, however, though he is very much concerned to establish certain general principles, rhythms, or patterns in his survey of civilization, does not fall into the error of underestimating the influence of creative minds and creative minorities. He even goes so far as to contend that the growth of civilization depends upon dynamic personalities, and includes in his third volume a series of vigorous sketches of personalities who have exercised this creative influence. We have pictures of St. Paul, of Mahomet, of Peter the Great and Thucydides, and curiously enough, of Emile Ollivier. The reason for the somewhat surprising inclusion of Emile Ollivier's name in such a list is not, of course, that he was a great originating political force (for he did not even make the Franco-Prussian war, nor could he have averted it), but because he illustrates 'the leitmotiv of withdrawal and return', which Professor Toynbee maintains to be, if not an invariable, at least a very general characteristic of great dynamic personalities. They withdraw themselves from the world and then return to it with their gifts and message etherealized. Thus Christ withdrew to the wilderness, thus St. Paul and Mahomet withdrew to the Arabian desert, thus the history of Thucydides, the *Divine Comedy* of Dante, and the immense autobiography of Ollivier are the fruit of enforced retirement from public affairs. No one will contest the value of a spell of real solitude and leisure for meditation in an active life. Especially is this true in the life of religious teachers. Yet there have been many dynamic personalities, towards the making of whose effective influence we can trace no such period of withdrawal. Napoleon is a case in point. His reflections in exile add little to his renown, and, though they were important in facilitating the return of his nephew to power, were posterior in time to the great achievement which transformed the institutions of France. There is also something to be said for Buffon's view that the note of a great career is 'the dream of youth executed in mature age'. If St. Paul's life was marked by a violent spiritual convulsion followed by a withdrawal, Darwin's was a long harmonious story of steady and continuous labour. The leitmotiv may be discerned in some, but not in all the creative lives of history.

One of the puzzles which meets the philosophic historian, who is anxious to bring all the facts within certain definite rubrics, is the capricious and apparently unaccountable appearance of men of genius. When a man of genius has arisen, the historian is able to trace the causes which facilitate or obstruct the spread of his influence. What no one has yet succeeded in doing is to account for his emergence at all. Why was Athens favoured and not Corinth, why Miletus and not Ephesus, why Florence and not Genoa, why have certain countries or centuries been barren of individual eminence and others poor? The historian can never wholly satisfy himself that his answer to these conundrums is correct.

Professor Toynbee's work is so rich in knowledge and suggestion that it is impossible to give a fair account of its contents within the space of a brief article. Wherever he ranges—and he goes everywhere —he has something to say which is fresh and arresting. The religion of the European races is a case in point. We know something now, thanks to the labours of Sir Arthur Evans, of the Minoan cult. We know that it was largely monotheistic and that the female form of divinity held the supreme place. We know, also, that the Zeus in Crete is nursed by nymphs, suckled by a beast in the field, and dies. All this leads Professor Toynbee to ask whether the Greek mysteries were not a survival of the religion of that Minoan world of which we have so recently discovered many brilliant monuments.

The Greek mysteries lead us to Christianity. Was there not much in the Christian doctrine as it was preached by St. Paul, or in the story of the life of Christ as it is presented in the Gospels, which responded to those elemental forms in the religious imagination of Mediterranean man which can be traced back to Minoan times? Here is Professor Toynbee's commentary on the Christian story:

In the story of Jesus, the Withdrawal-and-Return motiv perpetually recurs. Jesus is the babe born to a royal heritage —a scion of David or a son of God Himself—who is cast away in infancy. He comes down from Heaven to be born on Earth; he is born in David's own city of Bethlehem yet finds no room in the inn and has to be laid in a manger, like Moses in his ark or Perseus in his chest. In the stable, he is watched over by friendly animals, as Romulus is watched over by the wolf and Cyrus by the hound, and as Bellerophon is befriended by Pegasus; and he also receives the ministrations of shepherds, and is reared by a foster-father of humble birth, like Romulus and Cyrus and Oedipus. Thereafter he is saved from Herod's murderous design by being taken away privily to Egypt, as Moses is saved from Pharaoh's murderous design by being hidden in the bulrushes, and as Jason is placed beyond King Pelias' reach by being hidden in the fastness of Mount Pelion, and Cyrus beyond King Astyages' reach by being banished to the highland marches of Media. And then, at the end of the story, Jesus returns, as the other heroes return, to enter into His Kingdom. He enters into the King-dom of Judah when, riding into Jerusalem, He is hailed by the multitudes as the Son of David. He enters into the Kingdom of Heaven in the Ascension.

In all this, the story of Jesus conforms to the common pattern of the story of the foundling babe; but in the Gospels the underlying motiv of Withdrawal-and-Return presents itself in other shapes as well. It is present in each one of the successive spiritual experiences in which the divinity of Jesus is progressively revealed. When Jesus becomes conscious of His mission upon His baptism by John, He withdraws into the wilderness for forty days and returns from His Temptation there in the power of the spirit; 'and they were astonished at his doctrine, for his word was with power', 'for he taught them as one having authority, and not as the Scribes'. Thereafter, when Jesus realizes that His mission is to lead to His death, He withdraws again into the 'high mountain apart' which is the scene of His Transfiguration and returns from this experience resigned and resolved to die. Thereafter, again, when He duly suffers the death of mortal man in the Crucifixion He descends into the tomb in order to rise immortal in the Resurrection. And, last of all, in the Ascension, He withdraws from Earth to Heaven in order to 'come again with glory to judge both the quick and the dead: whose kingdom shall have no end'.

These crucial recurrences of the Withdrawal-and-Return motiv in the story of Jesus likewise have their parallels. The withdrawal into the wilderness reproduces Moses' flight into Midian; the Transfiguration on the 'high mountain apart' reproduces Moses' transfiguration on Mount Sinai; the death and resurrection of a divine being is anticipated in the Hellenic Mysteries and is derived by the Mysteries themselves from the world-wide agrarian ritual and myth; the tremendous figure who is to appear, and dominate the scene, at the catastrophe which is to bring to an end the present mundane order, is anticipated in the Zoroastrian Mythology in the figure of the Saviour (Saosyant) and in the Jewish Mythology in the figures of the Messiah and 'the Son of Man'. There is, however, one feature in the Christian Mythology which seems to have no precedent; and that is the interpretation of the future coming of the Saviour or Messiah or 'Son of Man' as the future return to Earth of an historical figure who has already lived on Earth the life of a human being. In this flash of intuition, the timeless past of the Foundling Myth and the timeless present of the Agrarian Ritual are translated into the historical striving of Mankind to reach the goal of human endeavours, or, on a wider than human range, into the unceasing travail of creation. In the concept of the Second Coming, the motiv of Withdrawal-and-Return attains its deepest spiritual meaning.

For these doctrines spreading among the Syriac and Greek proletariat of the Roman Empire there was the surer future, because, together with some elements of arresting novelty, they have much that was drawn from the age-long religious experience of the Mediterranean peoples. One reason, then, for the success of Christianity was that it held in solution so much that was ancient and indeed immemorial. Another reason was that the Church was self-governing. The Churches' hold over the affections and the allegiance of 'the internal proletariat' was far greater than the Emperor's hold over either portion of the proletarian underworld, because the Church had been established by the internal proletariat themselves out of their own spiritual and material resources.

The fall of the Roman Empire, in Gibbon's phrase, was 'the triumph of barbarism and religion'. Nobody has ever attempted to belittle the importance of Christianity as a factor of civilization. What, however, of the barbarians? The German school of his-

torians has not unnaturally exalted the Teutonic contribution, and Guizot himself in his famous book has
attributed to the Teuton conquerors of the Roman
Empire the introduction of the great and vivifying
principle of personal liberty. To this exaltation of
the *Völkerwanderung* as a fruitful source of institutions Professor Toynbee, with perhaps some excess
of conviction, offers a strong opposition. He points
out that, with the exception of Wessex and Austrasia,
all the barbaric successor states perished by violence.
'The barbarians', he writes, 'were not the assassins
of the mighty dead. They were merely the vultures
feeding on the carrion. Their heroic age was an
epilogue to Hellenic history, not a prologue to ours.
Their epic is a Swan Song.' Shades of Waitz and
Dahn, of Freeman and Stubbs! How far have we
not travelled since the days when we crowded to
Bayreuth to hear Wagner's *Ring*, and were taught that
in the dooms of the Anglo-Saxon kings was to be
found the kernel of English liberty.

The triumph of Islam in the East is attributed to the
fact that it was a non-Hellenic form of monotheism
specially suited to the Syriac civilization. Mahomet
did not work on a *tabula rasa*. He drew his inspiration
from Judaism and from Nestorianism, both of which
religions were Syriac. Islam, therefore, is 'a universal
Church originating in a form that was indigenous,
whereas Christianity was a universal Church originating in a form which was alien to the society in which
the Church played a part'. The Nestorian and Mono-
physite heresies were protests against the Hellenizing

of Christianity. They failed entirely to gain a hold in the West, but were a good deal more popular in the East. Even here, however, their success was limited and partial. Nobody pretends that the Nestorians of Assyria or the Copts of Egypt exercise a powerful religious influence on the world. They are, in Professor Toynbee's phrase, 'fossils'. Both these forms are eclipsed by Islam, 'a totalitarian Syriac religion anti-hellenic *au fond*'. The very fact that Christianity was so largely hellenized helped it in the West and hindered it in the East.

The Syriac civilization is distinguished for three facts. It gave mankind the Alphabet, it discovered the Atlantic ocean, and it invented monotheism. It is very largely to the Syriac element that Professor Toynbee is inclined to assign the brilliance of the Abbasid Caliphate, that second great Arab empire, with its capital at Bagdad, which made a social unity out of the two areas—one originally conquered from the Romans, and the other from the Sassanids which had been united politically under the Umayad régime. The Caliphate was successful because it was a reunion of territories primarily united under the Achaemenids, a reintegration or resumption of the Achaemenian Empire. But of the two elements so fused, the Iranian and the Syriac, it was the Syriac which was most important for culture. Was it not the inspiration of the Prophet himself, and the link which cemented Bagdad with the Arab-speaking world of the West?

It is no matter of surprise that a writer of Professor Toynbee's generation should have a very tempered

enthusiasm for the doctrine of nationality which inspired our fathers. It is clear that he considers the
war of Greek Independence to have been a mistake.
His contention is that if it had not been for Greek
(and presumably Serbian and Bulgarian) nationalism
the Balkans would have settled down quietly under
the Turkish régime, which was not only compatible
with a great deal of indolent toleration, but actually
encouraged the Phanariots (Phanar was the Greek
quarter in the north-eastern corner of Stamboul) to
carry on the most important tasks of government.
While the Phanariots were merchants on a large scale,
while they managed the affairs of the Greek Patri-
archate, and after 1883 obtained great offices of state,
what need was there for a revolution? As a result of
the nationalist wars 'an association of occupational
castes was cruelly rough-hewn into a congeries of
territorial nations'. Of the cruelty there can, unfortunately be no doubt; but a strong case can be made
for the conclusion that as a result of a long and terrible
story a higher standard of public life and general
security now prevails in the Balkans than could ever
have been reached under the Hamidian régime. The
idea that there is a necessary religious antagonism
between Greeks and Turks is properly dismissed by
Professor Toynbee, who reminds us that the Volga
Turks, 'who are distinguished by their sobriety,
honesty, thrift, and industry', live on the best of
terms with their Russian peasant neighbours. It is
also a hopeful sign (unnoted by Professor Toynbee)
that fifty Turkish boy scouts actually attended the

festivities in celebration of the centenary of Greek Independence.

There is so much that is excellent and stimulating in Professor Toynbee's study that it seems ungrateful to carp. One observation of a critical character, however, may be advanced. The generalizations are sometimes overdriven. It is, for instance, a perfectly sound point to urge that march-land territories, such as Brandenburg and Austria, or the frontier lands of Alexander the Great's empire, having a very special and arduous function to perform, are likely to be strongly organized and maintained. But is it a fair comment upon the course of events to say, 'Poland and Sweden both flourished so long as they fulfilled the functions of anti-Russian marches of the Western society; they began to decline towards their fall as soon as Russian Orthodox Christendom had achieved the *tour de force* of filching this function from them'? The causes of the decline of Poland and Sweden in the eighteenth century are familiar—the paralysing feuds of the Polish Diet, the mad adventures of a Swedish king. That the entry of Russia into Western politics exercised a prejudicial effect upon these two countries is true, but not inevitable. Other policies might have produced other results.

Again, we all, I hope, admire the Swiss. We admire their independence, and the way in which they have combined in one unity different races, languages, and religions. But is it not a little excessive to say of Switzerland (Venice and Holland are coupled with it in this connexion) that it has 'stimulated its inhabi-

tants to attain the highest levels of social achievement
that have yet been attained by any of the peoples of
Western Christendom'?

It is, of course, possible, again, that Professor Toynbee's account of the fact that Scandinavian civilization achieved its greatest triumphs in Iceland is correct
—i.e. 'transmarine migration across arctic seas, and
the exchange of a bleak and barren country-side in
Norway for an Icelandic country-side which was
bleaker and barrener'. But a great number of other
reasons suggests themselves, some of which seem to be
less recondite, such as that a number of families of
brilliant ability migrated to Iceland and there found
more leisure for literary pursuits. Again, I remember
meeting an old lady in Paris who had spent most of
her life in Greenland. She thought very little of Paris,
but was enthusiastic about Greenland, its tranquillity
and emptiness, its great air-washed spaces, its long,
quiet winter nights. She talked as if Greenland were
a veritable Capua. My venerable friend would not
have agreed with Professor Toynbee's suggestion that
the challenge of Greenland to the Norsemen might
have been too severe.

One of the dangers of 'pattern history', if it may be
so described, is that facts must be woven into the
pattern. One of its advantages is that a good and
attractive pattern prints itself upon the memory. A
pattern, symmetrical, shapeful, repetitive, is easier to
carry in the mind than a narrative. The pattern historian is on the look-out for analogies and gathers them
from every quarter. Ulstermen and Incas, Prussians

and Icelanders, Ainus and Berbers, assemble in their legions under the ample canopy of Professor Toynbee's learning to point the moral and adorn the tale. There is, too, in the past not only pattern but rhythm. Our enthusiastic guide is enchanted by the notion of rhythmical alternations of stability and movement, repose and turbulence, divine peace and diabolic unrest, which the Chinese designate under the names of Yin and Yang. In the great operatic performance of humanity he detects the recurrence of this leitmotiv of Yin and Yang. Other ears will be less sensitive to the regularity of the Chinese beat.

There are no dull pages. Though there is a good deal of discursive and pleasant rambling into theology, ethics, and literature, which leads us somewhat wide of the central argument, and a rich miscellany of citations from the Classics, Hebrew, Greek, Roman, German, and English, not to speak of many a curious page from modern travellers, and a fine piece of Greek elegiacs from the author's own pen to speed us on our way, there is no remission of intellectual tension and interest. The author has clear-cut convictions on a large number of things. He scolds Seleucus for establishing his capital at Antioch, and Charlemagne for drawing down the Scandinavian avalanche by his stupid resolve to conquer the Saxons, who, if left alone, would have succumbed to the peaceful penetration of the Christian missionaries. Perhaps Seleucus and Charlemagne might have prepared a tolerable defence. Who knows? Meanwhile, it is comfortable to have Professor Toynbee knowing so